CRITICAL STAGES of BIBLICAL COUNSELING

Getting Started:
The First Session

Breaking Through:
The Turning Point

Finishing Well:
The Termination

Jay E. Adams

Critical Stages
of Biblical Counseling

Contents

Critical Stages of Biblical Counseling

Introduction

I believe that apart from the publication of *Competent to Counsel* and *The Christian Counselor's Manual* this trilogy may be the most important and most helpful writing that I have done for counseling. In it I have tried to be as practical as I know how, introducing many matters that I have either not mentioned elsewhere or have treated only superficially. It is intended to be a substantial guide for novice and experienced counselors alike. I have attempted to take the reader through the actual process of dealing with matters encountered in the three most important counseling sessions in great detail. I have also attempted to outline the ways in which these sessions ought to be conducted. I have considered temptations and dangers that you are most likely to face. I have set forth a program for moving through these sessions with smoothness, thus avoiding the pitfalls most common to each. I have considered what to do when you fail; showing you how best to recoup. I have attempted to confront all of the major matters that pertain to each of the three sessions. I think that you will find this volume to be truly helpful. At any rate, I believe that you will be challenged by the plethora of issues that I have raised. May God use this trilogy, over which I have labored for many weeks, to bless you for many years to come!

CRITICAL STAGES
of BIBLICAL
COUNSELING

Getting Started
The First Session *of*
Biblical Counseling

Jay E. Adams

Getting Started
The First Session
of Biblical Counseling

Contents

Introduction

In the process of counseling, there are usually three points at which what happens in the session is critical. These are the first session, the turning point session, and the terminating session. It is not that other sessions are unimportant, but what happens at one or more of these points ordinarily determines the present and future outcomes of counseling. Each of these three sessions, therefore, deserves special attention. Because they are so important in the process of counseling, I have devoted a book to each session. This book, *Getting Started: The First Session of Biblical Counseling*, is the first of this trilogy.

The goal of this first book is to treat the first session more or less exhaustively, looking at what makes it important, how it ought to be conducted, what to expect, what to look for, and how to prepare for it. A good start is, as you may recognize, important to the success of any process. What is true generally is true especially of counseling. While it is not impossible to rectify a bad start by God's grace, it is much easier for all concerned to progress more surely and rapidly if there has been no need to recover and recoup. Therefore, helping to avoid flawed starts is one of the major reasons for writing this book. It would be difficult to underestimate the importance of the first session.

There are some who, as a rule, do not spend more than one session in counseling with anyone. It is their belief that to spend more time in counseling would be to imitate the secular counselor. At least two things may be said against this viewpoint. First, the amount of time necessary for doing biblical counseling is relatively small compared to the time spent in other sorts of counseling. But since change – even that change effected by the Spirit of God in sanctifying a believer – takes time, one may not ordinarily expect to achieve dramatic, complete, and lasting change in one session. Christian counseling is a ministry in which the goal is spiritual growth that honors the Lord; it is, therefore, an aspect of the sanctification process.[1] As in the

---

1 Growth takes time. There must be cultivation and maturation before fruit appears.

ministry of the Word in preaching, it takes instruction and regular, disciplined training over a period of time to effect significant change. So, too, in the ministry of the Word in counseling one must take the time for those things.

Second is that God, in the Scriptures, contemplates the regular use of multiple counseling sessions. In Titus 3:10, for instance, we read, "After confronting him in counseling once or twice, give up on a divisive person, and have nothing more to do with him" (CCNT). There would be little purpose to writing as he did if Paul did not consider counseling ordinarily to take several sessions. Here, however, because there is danger that a person intent on divisive action will split your congregation, he hurries matters up by limiting the number of sessions.[1] The idea is that if the offender doesn't come around in one or two sessions, then the counselor is directed to "give up" on him. The implication clearly is that Titus is not to do what he normally would do – take as many sessions as necessary to help a counselee to change. Under the special circumstance cited, however, if the counselee doesn't come around quickly – that is, in one or two sessions – he must be dismissed from the congregation. Church discipline, ordinarily a relatively slow process, must be accelerated. Paul tells the counselor that if change does not occur immediately, he must bring the counseling to a halt and "have nothing more to do with" the divisive person.

Paul is thinking of an emergency situation that must be handled in such a way as not to endanger the entire congregation.[2] In the non-emergency counseling context, where conditions are not so dependent upon a quick solution, the counseling would ordinarily take a number of sessions. Because it is an extraordinary counseling problem, I will not discuss divisiveness in this book beyond what I have said here. It is important, however, to note Paul's words to Titus, since from time to time such situations do develop. I can tell you only that when such a situation

---

1 But even then, he doesn't limit counseling to one session only.
2 All too often dismissal is postponed until it is too late; the offender eventually leaves anyway, but by then he usually takes others with him as well.

arose in a congregation that I was pastoring, I was grateful for the clear guidance of Paul's command in Titus 3. But even in the face of what Paul said, there still were persons who thought that we ought to have taken more time. Had we done so, we might have had an irreparable rift in the church.

So then, ordinary counseling is what I have in view in this book – if we can say that any counseling situation is ordinary! I have found that just when I think I have seen them all, and when I believe that I have most of the answers that are necessary, the Lord throws me a curve to keep me humble and to make me search even more deeply into His Word. I doubt but what He may do the same for you. There are, however, many commonalities in counseling cases. And when you confine your concerns to one of the three points of special concern that I have mentioned in depth, you will find that the number of commonalities will increase. So it is possible to anticipate many of those common circumstances and to be able to make helpful comments and suggestions about them. It is also helpful, as Paul did when writing to Titus about potentially divisive situations, to warn about problems that may arise at each point. Because these things are true, and because I have participated in literally hundreds of first sessions, I believe that I have some things to say that may steer you around a number of pitfalls and toward your goals instead.

So let's begin to explore the first session with hope and enthusiasm. What you do will set the tone for what follows – for good or for ill. It will help the counselee to gain confidence in your ministry to him and – what is of greater importance – in the Word of God and the God of the Word. What you do in the first session will help you to discover those things that will guide your counsel in the sessions that follow. And what you do in the first session will often determine whether the counselee will continue or not.

Chapter One

The First May Be the Last

I mean exactly what the title of this chapter implies – the first session may be the last session. The reason that I say this is to warn you that there are so many ways in which it is possible that counseling may not proceed beyond that point. Don't be surprised, then, if from time to time people show up for only one session. Counselors of all sorts find that this is so – not only biblical counselors. In addition to the reasons behind this phenomenon that are common to all counseling, there are special reasons why biblical counseling may cease after one session. I wish to consider some of those reasons in this chapter in order to help you forestall many of these potential desertions and thus reduce your number of truncated counseling cases. At any rate, knowing the facts should keep you from being surprised or totally frustrated when a case is cut short almost before it begins.

What are some of the reasons that counseling cases may be truncated after the first session? Fundamentally, the reasons fall into three categories:
1. The problem is solved in one session.
2. The counselee won't return.
3. You refuse to continue counseling (either temporarily or permanently).

I want to discuss each of those reasons separately.

To begin with, there *are* times when counseling takes no more than one session to complete. These are rare cases that usually involve providing information or giving simple direction. A counselee makes an appointment to discuss which college or university he should attend. Often the merits of the various options may be set forth in that one interview. However, there are dangers here. It is possible that in some instances, at least, the decision may be made on the basis of too little information. A second or third session may be very desirable. Don't determine too readily that such cases have been completed when you reach quick solutions. Quick solutions ought always remain suspect until you are sure that there is nothing more than is necessary for you to do. The counselee may need to be directed to gather more information (write for catalogs, speak to graduates, visit the campus and talk to the registrar) before making his decision. Assignments like these may require him to return for one or more sessions during which, in view of the materials gathered, you may discuss the matter more intelligently. Other seemingly simple sessions may need to be extended, typically to allow further data gathering.

Never close down counseling after one session if you have serious doubts. On the other hand, don't be too ready to extend counseling when the task truly has been completed. Sometimes, when you are not quite sure whether to conclude or not, tell the counselee, "Perhaps new data or new questions may arise after you leave this first session. I want you to feel free to call to arrange another session or two to discuss these matters." Assure the counselee that this sort of thing is not unusual, and that he should not hesitate to call. Indeed, if you strongly suspect that important questions may arise and that the counselee may be reluctant to call again, *you* may arrange a second visit. In doing so, you might suggest that the matter "may take a bit more time to jell, and that it is therefore desirable to discuss it further after gathering more information, praying, and sleeping on it for a few days." The key here is to make it absolutely clear to the counselee that additional sessions are nothing unusual, and that, indeed, they may be very important.

There are other situations in which one is called upon to make decisions (to move, to marry a certain person, to change jobs, etc.) in which the counselee is simply anxious to bounce the possibilities off another person whom he respects. Again, as mentioned above, only one session may be necessary (or, at times, no more are possible since a decision must be made immediately), but be sure that is true.

Often, when a counselee has discussed the various biblical options that lie before him (and, of course, as a biblical counselor, that is your prime concern), questions about the meaning or application of the scriptural passages that you used may surface after he leaves your office. Suggest this possibility to your counselee and encourage him to write these down to bring with him at a later time in a second session (or to ask about over the phone at a time agreeable to you both[1]).

The whole point of what I am saying is this: while there certainly are times when all that a counselee needs is the help that one session affords, concluding after the first session may be premature. So both you and he should feel perfectly free to schedule a return visit. The danger here is that because you are busy, you may be relieved to think no more sessions are needed. He may be overconfident and glad that there is no need to return. The tendency, in those situations, is to cut counseling short. But you must keep yourself from succumbing to this tendency. Each counselee deserves full attention. Indeed, if he does not receive it preventively, it is possible that later on you may find yourselves engaged in prolonged counseling sessions that grow out of hasty decisions.

On the other hand, there are persons who simply want to drag out counseling sessions when it is unnecessary to prolong them. The facts are clear, no more are needed, so the decision to terminate counseling should be made. But the counselee may want to come again and again – and perhaps even again! He or she[2] may be lonely, and may simply enjoy talking to a sympathetic person. Or the counselee may be one of those people who has difficulty making decisions – about *anything*. In such cases, the counselee must be taught the importance of becoming more decisive. Indeed, there are times when, for his own good, the counselee must be exhorted to make the decision and begin to follow through with it at this very session. However, there are some who need further counseling, not to discuss the matter that

---

1 Assuming that the questions do not involve a long discussion or are not intricate.
2 Male counselors should be wary of lonely women who wish to extend counseling.

occasioned counseling, but in order to discuss this very problem of decision making. That is better done not at the succeeding session, but at a later time. Do not confuse the two issues.

There are, of course, many other reasons that there would be no need for more than one counseling session. But in all of them, evaluate whether it might be advisable to schedule a follow-up session. It is often wise to do so, or at least to suggest to the counselee that he may need to make a further appointment after giving more thought to the matter.

As I said, the first session truly may be the last session because the problem is solved, because the counselee refuses to return, or because you refuse to counsel further. We have dealt with the first of these three reasons and will now turn to the second

Counselees may refuse to return to counseling even though you have scheduled another session. Many will phone on the day of the appointment to say that they are not planning to come. It would be good for you to alert your secretary to this possibility and to give her instructions about how to handle such calls. Here is one possible scenario:

—Hello. Pastor Smith's office. This is Jennifer speaking. How may I help you?

—Hello, Jennifer. This is Mrs. Jones. I'm afraid that I won't be able to make it to counseling today.

—Oh? Can you tell me why, Mrs. Jones?

—Well, I'm just not feeling up to it.

—Dr. Smith says this is one of the best times for you to come. You don't want to miss the special opportunity that this provides. If you hurry, you can make it on time.

Obviously, other scenarios will differ, but the secretary ought to be taught how to keep people from saying "no." You ought to insist that unless the counselee has a broken leg, or its equivalent, she ought to keep the appointment. You may have her stress that you have set aside this time especially for her (him), and that you turned away others who might have used it profitably. She may stress the importance of keeping one's word, the need to return to complete what was only begun, or other such matters. In each instance, she should maintain a cheerfully firm attitude. While not lecturing counselees, she should press upon them the need to come.

Counselees sometimes refuse to return because they recognize that you will expect them to make life changes in accordance with the Scriptures. Counselees may recognize that change will be required, and that change may be difficult. Even the idea of change may be challenging. It may involve doing things that counselees have never done before or things that they don't want to do. In such cases they must be encouraged, but also warned that refusal to do as God requires will bring only greater difficulty and heartache to all concerned. Tell them that it is a serious matter to deliberately refuse to do as God commands. You may have to ask them convicting questions like, "Are you prepared to tell *God* 'No'?"

There are, however, times when counselees misunderstand. They do not realize that to fail to do what is required is disobedience.[1] There may be occasions when you must spend time explaining what a passage of Scripture means and exactly how it applies. Even then, they may have doubts about the correct interpretation of verses and principles that are in question. In all such cases it will be necessary to spend time explaining. Indeed, it may take time at the end of the first session, time during a second session (if you can convince him to come and discuss matters), or time on the phone to effect this.

In addition to this problem, you will discover that some do not want to continue counseling because they fear doing what God may require of them, or they don't want to return out of fear of failure. Fear is a frequent factor in failure. Assure those who fear they will fail that God will give the wisdom and the strength to do as He commands. These usually come "in the

---

1 Always distinguish between what the Bible requires and your implementation of it. You may command the former, while you may only suggest the latter.

doing," as James says (James 1:25), not before. So excuses like "I don't think that I could do that," are invalid. Tell them, "What God requires, He provides the strength to accomplish. You may have failed before and I know that it hurts to have your hopes smashed. But this time it will be different because you will be following God's Word. If you do as He tells you there, you may be sure that He will not let you fail." It may take some convincing to get fearful counselees to assent. Presenting biblical promises in ways that make it clear that what you are saying is not your word but God's is vital to eliciting commitment. Always direct your counselees' faith and trust toward God's Word – not toward yours.

Then there are those who don't like the homework assignment that you gave, and because they didn't do it, don't want to return. They think that it will be embarrassing to face you. Tell your secretary to explain to them that you would like to have an opportunity to further discuss the homework *helpfully,* and that it is important to come for that reason alone. Have her explain that failure to do homework often uncovers other problems that may be more basic than the ones that the counselee presented at the outset. Homework failure, then, can be very valuable to you, the counselor. When you investigate what it was that kept the counselee from doing it, you may discover that he is disorganized, that he misunderstands directions, that he is lazy, that he gets sidetracked by other interests, or that he thinks he has a better way than God's way. The number of valuable discoveries that may arise from examining homework failure is vast. Search them out diligently. In them, you will often find the underlying cause of the problem or problems that you were originally asked to help solve. At all costs, then, do everything you can to get counselees to come in spite of their failure to do homework.

Some counselees will simply dig in their heels at doing what the Bible commands. For instance, there are those who refuse to break up an adulterous affair, even though they admit to it and agree that God would have them do so. Others will not seek forgiveness for some sinful action toward another person – and on, and on. In such cases, it is important to let the counselee know that this rebellious attitude, if it persists, will lead to church discipline. To explain fully what that means – especially as it may lead to being put out of the church – is essential. Most do not understand that being "handed over to Satan" involves the possibility of enduring physical trials at his hand that may end in "the destruction of the flesh" (I Corinthians 5:5).[1]

Certainly, this is the most discouraging aspect of the one-time session, and it is one that you will do everything possible to avoid. Pray for and with a counselee who refuses to return. Make more than one attempt to change his mind; you may want to send an elder of the church to speak with him if necessary. Sometimes you will succeed. But you will not win them all. Be sure of that. Some one-session counseling cases will remain one-session cases no matter what you do.

We turn now to the third reason that the first session may be the last – you may be the one who terminates counseling. "Why," you may ask, "would you ever think of doing that?" There are many reasons, some of which I shall mention here.

For one thing, if church discipline – which I have just mentioned – is required, it may be absolutely necessary to bring the session to a halt while the church carries out the process. You may be the one who must initiate the discipline. If counseling has turned up problems that involve repaying money stolen from another, which the counselee refuses to repay, for instance, counseling may take a quite different turn.

If a counselee makes demands of you that you cannot biblically meet, even after you've made every attempt to convince him to alter those demands, then you may simply have to refuse further counseling. He may, for instance, ask you to keep quiet about an affair he is having and not tell his wife. Confidentiality in biblical counseling is not absolute. The agreement that a counselee signs when he enters upon counseling should clearly state that you will keep matters as confidential as the Bible requires, but that this does not mean absolute confidentiality. Also, in any such agreement, there should be a clause stating

---

1 Please see my book *A Handbook of Church Discipline* for details.

that the counselee understands that the interpretations of the Bible guiding the counseling process are to be those of the counselor.

Another reason to stop counseling: you may require a certain response from the counselee that is not forthcoming, without which you *cannot* go on. Counseling must, therefore, cease until such a response is given. For instance, you may insist that before counseling proceeds, the counselee must agree to the document that I have just mentioned. He may not wish to do so. In another case, you may give a homework assignment to "bring in a list of all the ways that you are failing God as a person, as a husband and as a father." The counselee may balk at this assignment, though you believe that it is essential to making any progress at all. Until the counselee agrees to do the assignment, counseling may have to end. In a third instance, you may call off counseling because the counselee is not interested in biblical change, but only in getting relief. He may tell you so in no uncertain terms. Finally, because a would-be counselee plainly says that he is not a Christian, you may have to tell him that you cannot counsel him until he becomes a Christian.[1] That is because he cannot make changes that are pleasing to God (Romans 8:8[2]), and you refuse to help him make changes that displease Him.

In general, then, it is important to understand that, either permanently or temporarily, the first session may be the only session. That is sad in those situations that call for multiple sessions, but it is sometimes all you may hope for. Do your best to overcome resistance to further sessions if and when they are required. But, as I said, you will not win them all.

---

1 Though you will be glad to speak to him about how he may be saved.
2 "Those who are in the flesh [unbelievers] cannot please God."

Chapter Two
Put First Things First

Nothing is more important than the atmosphere in which counseling is done. I am not referring to what many counselors think most important – a permissive, accepting atmosphere – but to an atmosphere in which everything, from the outset, plainly speaks of the fact that this counseling will be carried on in the presence of God. In all that you do and say, you are obligated to bring the counselee and His God into confrontation with each other. This sort of atmosphere should exude respect for God and His Word, an obvious concern to honor and please Him, and a willingness to adhere to what Scripture says without any hesitation or fudging. As a Christian counselor you can have no lesser objective. Any other sort of atmosphere cannot rightly be called "Christian counseling."[1]

It is one thing to have such an objective in one's heart – as good as that may be; it is another to create an atmosphere that is equally conspicuous to counselees. There are counselors who will affirm all of what I said above about their objectives, who either are afraid to make this clear to their counselees or who do not know how to do so. This chapter's purpose is to challenge fearful counselors[2] and to help those who simply do not know how to bring about a truly Christian atmosphere.

Let's understand that God is our environment, as I showed in my book *The Theology of Counseling*. Even if we wanted to, we could not escape Him. Psalm 139:1–18 (NASB) expresses this fact powerfully:

1 O LORD, You have searched me and known me.
2 You know when I sit down and when I rise up;
You understand my thought from afar.
3 You scrutinize my path and my lying down,
And are intimately acquainted with all my ways.

---

1 Though there is much counseling done under that label that has little resemblance to anything Christian.
2 Are you one of them?

17

4   Even before there is a word on my tongue,
    Behold, O LORD, You know it all.
5   You have enclosed me behind and before,
    And laid Your hand upon me.
6   Such knowledge is too wonderful for me;
    It is too high, I cannot attain to it.
7   Where can I go from Your Spirit?
    Or where can I flee from Your presence?
8   If I ascend to heaven, You are there;
    If I make my bed in Sheol, behold, You are there.
9   If I take the wings of the dawn,
    If I dwell in the remotest part of the sea,
10 Even there Your hand will lead me,
    And Your right hand will lay hold of me.
11 If I say, "Surely the darkness will overwhelm me,
    And the light around me will be night,"
12 Even the darkness is not dark to You,
    And the night is as bright as the day.
    Darkness and light are alike to You.
13 For You formed my inward parts;
    You wove me in my mother's womb.
14 I will give thanks to you, for I am fearfully
        and wonderfully made;
    Wonderful are your works,
    And my soul knows it very well.
15 My frame was not hidden from You,
    When I was made in secret,
    And skillfully wrought in the depths of the earth;
16 Your eyes have seen my unformed substance;
    And in Your book were all written
    The days that were ordained for me,
    When as yet there was not one of them.
17 How precious also are Your thoughts to me, O God!
    How vast is the sum of them!
18 If I should count them, they would outnumber the sand.
    When I awake, I am still with You.

Wherever one may happen to be is also where God is, because He is omnipresent (everywhere at the same moment). Christian counselees usually know this as a fact they have been taught.

But frequently they need to be reminded of the reality of it. That is one of the main reasons for creating an atmosphere in which the truth of this Psalm is apparent. By the way in which one conducts counseling, by the place he gives to Scripture as his authority, and by the concern he expresses to do all in accordance with biblical teaching, the counselor manifests his belief in what the Psalmist wrote.[1]

It is important for the counselee to receive counsel in such an atmosphere. When he does, he will be thinking about his life in relationship to others, not merely in terms of how counseling will affect him or them, but primarily about how he will please or displease God. That is what biblical counselors want to achieve in counseling – a situation in which counselees seek to do God's will rather than merely get relief from some problem. Too often, your counselee may arrive full of the relief-orientation. The atmosphere in which he finds himself in your counseling room, however, should go far toward bringing about a change in which his emphasis upon self shifts to an emphasis on God. Atmosphere alone, of course, cannot do this, but it can contribute to such a change. How does one bring about this kind of God-pervasive atmosphere in counseling? I can mention only a few items here.

First, not only must the counselor consciously work at creating this atmosphere, but he must himself also desire it in all that he does. He must have genuinely Christian concerns. That means this atmosphere must be present in his preparation for counseling, in his studies and prayer outside of the counseling room, and in the way he conducts himself while counseling.

Consider the last of these three items. Your language, for one thing, must be largely the language of the Scriptures – certainly not the language of the psychologists and psychiatrists. You should speak of God in familiar terms (you must not be embarrassed to do so, the way some are). This language, incidentally, will indicate that you are more interested in what God does in counseling sessions than in what you yourself do. In

---

1 Of course, he must not do this for show; he must truly mean every bit of it.

every way, you should want your speech to direct the counselee to think of God rather than of himself. You will say things like, "So you see this is what God thinks of that idea," rather than "*I* think that this idea is..." You will back up your suggestions, thoughts, and homework assignments with biblical support. You will do this not as so many do, by trying to find verses to support their own ideas (thereby often distorting their plain meaning), but by *deriving* your ideas from the Bible through careful exegesis. Then you will "open" the Scriptures for counselees as you explain and apply the Scripture to the situation at hand. You will attempt to do that in ways that make it clear to the counselee that what you are saying is exactly what God said. You must desire to become a herald from God, an agent of Another who represents Him in counseling. In other words, you must recognize that the real Counselor is the Holy Spirit Who caused the Bible to be written and Who works through it as it is faithfully administered in God's Name. To put it simply, the biblical counseling atmosphere should exalt the Lord and His Word!

In accordance with all that has been said, the first session should be conducted in a workman-like atmosphere as well. There is hard work to be done for God; the way in which you counsel should also convey that fact. Counseling is not chit-chat. It is serious business, and those who are involved in it are there to accomplish what the Lord wants done. That does not mean that there can be no moments of laughter; please do not be dour or glum. But your laughter must contribute to the serious nature of the work at hand.

Serious counselors usually counsel from desks or tables; they do not sit in chairs facing the counselee as if they were there merely for conversational purposes. They have paper, pen, books and other materials ready for use – and they use them! The telephone is nearby in case its use is necessary. In other words, from the start, the counselee should be aware of the fact that the counselor is ready for work. Everything about the setting should indicate that the session will be a *working* session.

The third element that ought to pervade the atmosphere is a sense of hopefulness. There is every reason for you to expect good things to happen when God is at work in a counselee's life. Hope certainly will be communicated to the counselee when your attitude is proper. Indeed, counselees seem to have an uncanny way of detecting whether the counselor thinks there is hope for them or not.

Not only is it important for the counselor to communicate hope by speaking about God's promises with confidence; he must also believe that this is so. No other counselor can give the assurance that a Christian counselor can. Only he knows for sure that when counselees conform to the Scriptures, the promises of the Scriptures will be fulfilled. Indeed, he can actually *guarantee* that when they do so, God will do as He has promised. Moreover, he knows that by the use of the Word in the power of the Spirit every problem can be solved God's way (notice: I did not say "the counselee's way"). That is a wonderful expectation with which to begin counseling. Remind yourself of these facts before each session and enter into counseling with great expectations! If you don't, there is something wrong. Make sure that you always communicate enthusiasm for God and what He will do. If that is lacking, it is possible that you also need counseling.

I have tried to explain how the atmosphere in which the first session is conducted can make a great difference. Counselor, have you ever thought about these things before? If not, it is high time to do so, don't you think? But one word of caution: be sure that all of the things that I have been saying about atmosphere come from your heart. You cannot program counseling in a mechanical way; it is a matter of persons (the principal One of whom is God) responding and relating through the medium of the Bible. The decisions that are made, the knowledge that is gained, the actions that are taken must all flow from inner conviction. You and your counselee must realize that counseling is no charade before God but, rather, a real life drama that is played out in His presence, calling upon Him to bless and help throughout. Under those circumstances, the first session will be a glad harbinger of what is to come. Be sure, too, that this is true of each of your sessions thereafter, and not only of the first.

Chapter Three

What To Do First

What I have written in the previous chapter has to do with preparation – the preparation of the counselor as he invites counselees to participate in a proper biblical counseling atmosphere. This chapter, while no less important, deals with a different sort of preparation: preparation for counseling through the use of materials prior to counseling itself. I am referring to two valuable documents that the counselor's secretary asks the counselee to fill out prior to meeting with the counselor. These are the Personal Data Inventory (PDI) and the Counseling Agreement (CA). While neither is absolutely necessary (in that good counseling may be done without them), they not only save time for all concerned, but also assure that everyone knows beforehand what will be involved in counseling, thus avoiding unpleasant surprises or misunderstandings.[1]

The Personal Data Inventory

The Personal Data Inventory (PDI) as the name indicates, is a data-gathering tool. If you will turn to the copy of the PDI provided in the appendix (page 230), you will quickly gather by perusing it that this document covers pertinent information that would take almost one full session to obtain verbally. Many pastors think that to have a member of their church fill out a PDI is a waste of time. They believe that they already have the information it would retrieve. If you are one of them, I challenge you to try to fill out a PDI on any member of your congregation *yourself* and see how many blank spaces you leave! How many pastors, for instance, know what prescription drugs their parishioners are taking? Yet this may be vital information that has to do with the way they act. How many know whether their coun-

---

1 Or, in this litigious age, legal difficulties.

selee has been having sleep loss? But, again, this could be very applicable to bizarre behavior that a member may be exhibiting. And so it goes. I suggest, therefore, that you have *all* counselees fill in the PDI if you want an abundance of information quickly. Why waste time having to find out these things – and others – the hard way? Moreover, few counselors are organized enough to remember all the questions that the PDI asks; yet any one of, or any combination of, these questions neglected may lead to failure in counseling.

The PDI deals with two kinds of information:
1. Information specifically solicited by the counselor.
2. Information that the counselee offers in a more general way.

Both sorts of information, at different times and in separate ways, will prove valuable in the counseling process.

The former type of information concerns routine data such as name, address, phone number, age, number and age of family members, whether one is a Christian or not,[1] what church he attends and how often, whether or not he is taking any prescription drugs, and the like. Along with this routine information, other, more specialized, data is requested, such as whether one has used illicit drugs, has ever been arrested, or has had previous counseling or psychotherapy (and the outcome). In addition, there are questions designed to discover if he has perceptual problems[2] or shows signs of depression.[3]

The second section asks four general questions of the counselee. They are:

What is your problem?
What have you done about it?
What do you want us to do about it?
What further information about yourself should we know?

---

1 The answer to this question has to do with qualifying a person for counseling.
2 The nine questions beginning with "Have you ever thought people were watching you?"
3 This section begins with "the words that best describe you now" (stress the *now*).

These questions allow the counselee to set forth the situation as he sees it. The fourth is a catch-all designed to pick up extraordinary factors that the PDI may not have asked. The responses to these four questions can be most helpful. If a counselor elects to not use the rest of the PDI, I urge him at the very least to ask these last four questions at the outset of counseling.

Notice, none of these questions begins with the word "why." Why-type questions tend to put pressure on persons that may bring conviction, and were used by Jesus for that purpose in the gospels. But He never used them to gather data. What, when, where, how, and which type questions more readily bring forth data that is factual and not speculative.

Counseling will normally begin with the use of the answers found on the PDI. The secretary usually brings the two documents into the counseling room usually five minutes before admitting the counselee. The counselor looks over the PDI to discover whether there are any answers that require further elucidation. Typically, he will mark them with a highlighter so as to remember to explore them in this first session. An example of this might be a "yes" answer to "Have you ever been arrested?" The counselor will be interested in hearing more about this. He will ask the counselee to explain as the occasion warrants. An explanation that, "My wife had me locked up," together with the reasons that follow, often will throw much light on the current problem – particularly if it involves marital difficulties.

Consider another response, this time to the question "Have you had counseling or psychotherapy before?" If the answer is yes, and the list of occasions is numerous, but he explains that the results were not helpful, the counselor will surmise that the counselee may need to be given hope. Previous failures so discourage many counselees that they raise their guard against getting their hopes up again. Their expectations may be very low. Indeed, they may have come to counseling as a last hope, or even a hope against hope!

It is important to investigate what previous counselors may have said the problem was, what advice they gave, and what results followed taking that advice. This information may uncover new complicating problems that resulted from previous counseling, some of which can be as great as, or even greater than, the original problem. In such cases, undoing of wrongdoing will often be necessary. Sometimes you cannot "get at" the present problem until you first disentangle it from such complications.

One counselee was advised that his problem was his father. He was told by a previous, non-Christian counselor that it would help to "tell his father off." The counselee said that he couldn't because his father was dead. The counselor told him that this was no problem since he could get rid of his hostility by urinating on his father's grave. When the counselee followed this advice, the guilt that ensued was as great a problem as his previous one. And, of course, the counselee's problem was not his father, it was how he had learned to respond to him. In so responding to his father over the years, the counselee had developed sinful habit patterns that were still with him and according to which he was now dealing with others. The problem was in him. Regardless of how his father treated him – and later, it became uncertain whether the father was all that wrong after all – he had learned to deal with wrongdoing (or imagined wrongdoing) wrongly. He needed advice that would point to principles found in the book of First Peter rather than the advice to urinate on his father's grave.[1]

Having explored any items on the first list, the counselor will turn to the counselee's answers to the four questions on the second list. Normally, counseling begins with these. If, for instance, the answer to the second question, "What have you done about it [the problem]" is "I prayed," the counselor may wish at the proper time to ask, "What did you pray that God would give you the wisdom and strength to do about it?" This follow-up question will usually go unanswered, because that is not the way that the counselee looks at prayer. Many counselees believe that prayer is punting. That is to say, they think that once

---

1 See my books *Trust and Obey* and *The Christian Counselor's Commentary* on I Peter.

they have prayed, the ball is in God's hands and He must run with it. They then fail to look for any biblical commands that may be given to help them solve the problem. Instead, having prayed, they expect God to do everything. They are ignorant of what He has told them to do in the Scriptures. Responding to the counselee's answer in that way may open an entirely new avenue of approach for him. It will point him to the responsibilities that God expects him to assume in solving the problem. It will show him that prayer and biblically directed action are not antithetical. The solution is not a matter of either/or but of both/ and.

The first question, "What is your problem?" will elicit an answer on one of three levels. They are:

1. the level of irritation (what ails him, what drove him to counseling);
2. the level of the specific action or attitude behind this particular problem;
3. the level of the underlying pattern.

The answer at the first level may look like this: "I lost my job." At the second level, it may be: "I got into a fight with the boss and was fired." At the third level: "I have an ungovernable temper which led to being fired from my job." As you can see, all three are correct answers, but they get at different things. Too often, all you will receive is an answer at the first level – the level of irritation. In counseling, then, you will need to ask further questions to obtain answers at the next two levels (questions like "What happened?" in response to his level one response, and "Is this the only time that something like this has happened?" in response to a level two answer). Of course, it may have been the only time that anything of this sort has happened; there may be no level three pattern at all. If so, don't invent one! You will have enough to deal with at levels one and two as it is. But if there is an underlying pattern, you will have helped the counselee only minimally if you fail to uncover and deal with it. He will only return again (and again) later on when his temper gets the better of him in later instances. You need to handle his problem at all levels – not merely get him out of the current mess. Often, psychiatrists deal with problems at level one only by prescribing medication to alleviate the person's bad feelings. As you can see, that is not adequate. Many biblical counselors fail to investigate level three and instead help counselees solve only the immediate problem. Learn to examine all three levels. So how the counselee answers the question "What is your problem?" will determine what you will ask next.

The question "What do you want us to do about it?" is crucial. Here you are asking for the counselee's agenda. If he is interested only in relief, you will probably discover that by his answer to this question. Then you will have to move him to a greater motive: to please God whether relief comes or not.[1]

Often a counselee's agenda will be quite different from God's (which, of course, is the one that you, as His representative, must adopt). He may want "acceptance" of or "support" for his attitudes or actions. He may want you to "side" with him against his wife (or she against her husband). He may want you to help him "acquire a better self image." He may want you to declare his case is "helpless." These objectives are quite antithetical to what God would require of him. Therefore, before you go much further in counseling, you will have to negotiate his agenda. You will do this not to reach some compromise, as in a business negotiation, but to bring him into accord with a biblical agenda. When God's agenda and his clash, it is useless to go farther in counseling until the two agendas are brought into harmony. Otherwise, you will be working at cross purposes.

It is at this point that you may find it necessary to end or suspend counseling. If the counselee refuses to make the biblical agenda his own, but insists on sticking to an unbiblical one, you cannot go on. You may wish to discuss the matter fully with him or give him an assignment designed to show him God's objectives in a situation like his. But if he adamantly refuses to change his agenda so as to conform to God's, you will find it

---

1 That is, relief of the sort he wants. God always brings peace to those who do His will, but it is of His sort and comes in His time and His way.

necessary to terminate counseling (either permanently, or until the counselee comes around to God's way).

I could go on talking about the uses of the PDI. But you will discover various ways in which to use it for yourself. I believe that it is a valuable instrument for counseling purposes and strongly urge you to use it in each counseling case. Not only does it elicit information, but it serves other important purposes as well. It adds a more professional look to your counseling (this often helps counselees to get more serious about counseling), it prepares the counselee for the sorts of things that will be discussed in the sessions to follow and it helps him to think seriously, in a more structured manner, about what he will say when he enters the counseling room.

The Counseling Agreement

The Counseling Agreement (see Appendix 2, page 233) is an instrument that the secretary gives the counselee before he enters counseling. It is designed to protect both the counselor and the counselee, though it is weighted toward the counselor. It is important for the secretary (or the counselor, if need be) to explain any matters that the counselee may not understand. This need may arise, especially, with reference to matters of confidentiality. The counselee may want counseling data treated as if it were received in a confessional. He must understand that absolute confidentiality came from the Roman Catholic Church not from the Bible. There are many times when what is divulged in counseling must be related to others – even to the church, as Matthew 18:15 and following indicates. So a clause to this effect is altogether appropriate. In this day of lawsuits, it is important to protect the interests of the church, its members, and the counselors who minister to them. Therefore, I urge you to use this form or some variation of it that fits your particular situation. There is no need to discuss its contents, as what it says is self-evident.

The Weekly Counseling Record

In Appendix 3 (page 234), you will find a Weekly Counseling Record (WCR). This is a record that the counselor uses each week in the counseling session, on which he takes notes and lays out objectives for the future (the latter in the agenda column[1]). He records not only the drift of the session but the results of the previous week's assignments. Of course, in the first session, he will have no information for this section. He may use it, instead, to record any special information that is obtained from the PDI that he wants to highlight for present or future reference.

Keeping careful records can be of great value in counseling. If a counselee says, "This is the sixth session and I don't think that we are getting anywhere," you can lay out the records for the previous five sessions and detail what sorts of problems have been solved and what progress has been made. ("Look, back here. Four weeks ago we were struggling with getting a new job. You now have it. We are currently working on the pattern of losing your temper. That's progress.") On the other hand, if the counselee is not making progress as he (or she) should, the same records can be used to make out that sort of case as well.

These records can also provide a tailor-made prayer list for the counselor each week. You will discover that accurate records help you remember what you might have otherwise forgotten. Sometimes counselees will need to return for counseling after several years. To have records to review will help immensely on such occasions. Be sure that in leaving a pastorate, you take those records with you. They are your records; you do not want others viewing them. Moreover, a coding system (numbers for names, etc.) would be helpful to keep prying

---

1 Matters that arise in a session and that should be considered later should be noted in the agenda column of the WCR. Those dealt with should be checked off at the time. Those not handled in one session should be carried forward and written in the agenda column of succeeding WCRs until completed. Writing these in each week prior to the counseling session reminds you of items that you may wish to deal with this week.

members out of your records if for some reason they should want to read them. The danger of this should be apparent; so under ordinary circumstances, records should be kept under lock and key. But, even with that precaution, all sorts of unforeseen circumstances may arise in which you would be well-advised not to have names recorded.

So, as you can see, in careful counseling the biblical counselor is concerned about preparation for the first session. When he develops a routine like the one described above, he will become much more confident and proficient because he knows what to do and how to go about accomplishing it. It is important for a counselor to be on top of things, to take a firm hand in guiding the counseling process, and to know what he needs to accomplish. These materials, used wisely, will help in this regard. In the next chapter I will enlarge on directing counseling in a confident manner.

Chapter Four

Who's In Charge?

That question is probably as crucial to settle during the first session as any. If the counselee gains control of the session, counseling is sure to founder. From the outset, therefore, the counselor must assert and maintain leadership in the counseling process. This is true especially of the first session, in which policies and practices are introduced and established.

There will be counselees who will attempt to take control of counseling. Some will try to lay down rules by which they think counseling should be conducted.[1] Others will tell you what topics they will discuss and which ones they will not.[2] In any number of ways, some counselees will make an effort to lead the counseling in the directions that they want it to go.

Not all attempts to gain control of counseling by counselees should be considered nefarious. Indeed, many times the counselee is so anxious to help that he allows his anxiety to overcome his better judgment. At other times, he may think that he knows the area into which counseling should move and will make serious attempts to keep it out of any other. While the motives of the counselee may be strictly aboveboard, the actions that he takes may hinder counseling. And when this happens, the counselor must tell him so.

In non-directive counseling and free association techniques, the counselor attempts to let the counselee control or direct the session. Quite the opposite is true of the biblical counselor. In kindly ways, he lets the counselee know that he is interested in all that the counselee has to say, but that it must be said in an orderly, systematic way. He will make it clear that the counselee

---

1 The "professional counselee," who is more interested in the process than in the result, more than likely will do so. Because he has lost hope in all counseling, he has become a counseling sampler instead of a genuine counselee.
2 See more on this in Chapter Eight, page 59.

is there because there are difficulties that he has not been able to solve on his own, and that part of his problem may be that he hinders others from helping by being too ready to tell them what to do (or how to do it).

The procedures in the previous chapter will help to establish that the counselor has a method for counseling, that he knows what he is up to and knows where he is going. In most cases, this in itself will establish his leadership in the session. Nevertheless, there will be times when counselees will still seek to gain control.

Let's take an example. Mary comes into the first session with many aspects of her problem on her mind. It has not occurred to her to write these down. So since she doesn't want to forget any of them, she begins to blurt out, "There is this situation with my husband and the kids, and I mustn't forget the problem with my mother-in-law! And...." As she continues, it immediately becomes apparent to the wise counselor that he must break into this recital and help. In a cheerful manner he says, "Whoa, Mary! All of those matters seem very important. I don't want to miss any of them. So take your time and let me write down each on my agenda column so that we can get to them one at a time in an orderly fashion. Now, let's see...." Mary will be relieved that she has gotten off her chest all of the items she has been trying to remember. Pleased with the promise that in due time each will be taken up and not forgotten, she can settle back, relax a little, and respond properly as the counselor takes up each item in order. I have even had counselees reach over and point a finger at some item I have written on my agenda list and say, "Be sure you get to this." My reply? "That's why I've written it down. At the proper time – in this session or in a later one – we'll take up the matter."

In Proverbs 18:15, the writer says, "A discerning mind gets knowledge and the ear of the wise seeks information" (Berkeley). The two verbs in the proverb are significant. In gathering data (which is one of the important tasks for the counselor in the early sessions) he will see to it that he "seeks" and "gets" the data that he needs since he is anxious to learn all he can about the case. He will not allow the counselee to rush him into a quick decision about any matter or to move on to another before he has finished with the first. In the same chapter, Proverbs 18:13, he is instructed that "He who answers before he hears, it is a folly to him and a reproach" (Berkeley). Biblical counselors, in taking heed, should be careful not to follow foolish ways for which they may deserve reproach. That is one reason why they are cautious about allowing others to tell them what to do in counseling. They have a method for gathering all the pertinent information and they will pursue it. They will not allow a counselee to pressure them into abandoning it. Of course, that does not mean that they are utterly inflexible. Certainly, they will listen to reason, but the reason must be a very good one to cause them to pursue some other approach. There will be very few instances in which this is likely to happen.

But what is the counselor's method? It is the extensive/intensive method. Biblical counselors want to find out all that they can about the counselee so that they don't give counsel on the basis of too little information. Proverbs 18:13, just mentioned, looms large in their thinking.[1] So they ask about matters all around the circle of the counselee's life. If the life of a counselee is thought of in terms of a pie in which each slice stands for a segment (his physical life, his business life, his family life, his social life, his church life – that last slice is not his relationship to God; God is over the entire pie!), then the counselor may ask a number of pertinent questions about each of these areas, noting which answers seem to be hot spots to be revisited later more intensively.[2] Having completed the inventory of each area (and it would be good to have standard questions to ask about each, as well as questions that seem important from the PDI and other information offered by the counselee), he may then move

---

1 They might do well to place Proverbs 18:13, 15, 17 under the glass on their desks.

2 He determines this not only by the content of what is said, but by halo data (non-verbal expressions of voice or body) and by obvious attempts to avoid certain matters, etc.

on to intensive questioning.[1] Here he asks detailed questions growing out of the responses he elicited from the counselee during extensive questioning. As answers to these more detailed questions are given, he may wish to write down in his agenda column other matters they suggest which he will take up later. It is not wise to allow the counselee to offer other suggested ways of gathering the information. Nor should counselors allow any interruptions that would delay the completion of the process. A good counselor knows what he wants to "get," and he "seeks" it. That means, in counseling, he has developed a method and will use it. Naturally, you may wish to modify the method that I have suggested in various ways (slicing the pie into more slices, for instance) but be sure that whatever you do covers a person's entire life.

Why should we cover a person's entire life? After all, the problem may be in his business area. Why not focus on that alone? Indeed, that may be the sort of thing that the counselee wonders about too. Here's why: we are whole persons. When things go wrong in one segment of his life, this may affect him in other areas as well. If things aren't going well at work, he may become hard to live with at home. In time, that will lead to problems there. Difficulties in any segment, left unresolved over time, have a way of permeating the whole of a person's life. So the problem may not be only a problem at work, it may have affected his home life, his physical life (losing sleep over the work difficulties), or even his social and church life. Because old, unresolved problems often lead to new problems, it is unwise not to investigate all areas of a counselee's life.

Establishing leadership in the first session is important for establishing it in sessions to come. If you lose control of the first session, it will be hard to gain it back in succeeding ones. Moreover, a counselee may sense that the session is out of your control and may become discouraged by this. That can be true even when he unconsciously sets stumbling blocks in this regard before the counselor. Be blunt in a cheerful, kindly way about

---

1 This may take more than one session to cover adequately.

this issue of leadership whenever it is the only way to obtain it. You may have to say, "You know, John, it isn't easy to gather information when you keep trying to change the subject. Let's get back on track and stay there or we may never get to the bottom of the problem. Okay?" Securing a commitment by throwing out that "Okay" challenge to him may also help. Should he fail to keep it, you can always refer to it in the future: "John, remember, you agreed not to interrupt the flow of our investigation. Now, let's get back on track again."

In another instance, a husband may begin addressing his wife in a contradictory and hostile manner. She, in turn, may attempt to answer in kind. In some cases, they may even yell or make derogatory remarks. The counselor will not allow this kind of behavior. Instead, he will quickly assert his leadership, breaking in, saying something like this: "Bill. Peggy. Let me make a couple of things clear. One reason that you are here is because you talk that way to one another. The rule here is that we will talk and act like Christians should. If you have disagreements, talk to *me* about them, not to one another. You have not yet learned how to talk productively to one another. That will come in time, but for now, please address me."

If, after many such explanations, they continue to speak like that, you may have to curtail counseling until such time as they are willing to abide by the rules of the session.

If you cannot establish leadership in this session because the counselee insists on having it his way, you may have to bring the counsel to a screeching halt. Make it clear that you do not want to but that you find it impossible to continue under the present circumstances. You will be glad to attempt to do so at another time if and when the counselee has had time to think matters over and wants to follow your lead.

In none of this should the counselor act as if he knows it all. What he makes clear is that he has a way to proceed and that he cannot see any reason in this case to abandon that procedure. He wants to expedite the counseling and can only see the constant deviations as hindering and diverting the surest path to a solution.

Chapter Five

Giving Hope

It is useless to begin counseling with those who do not have hope. They will not persevere when the counseling becomes tedious or difficult. In I Thessalonians 1:3, Paul writes of "the endurance that comes from hope." The connection between hope and endurance is one with which every counselor should be familiar. Ordinarily, counselees will find it necessary to work hard at tasks that require regular, daily discipline to achieve. This can be tedious to those who have never learned disciplined living. Sometimes a counselee will be asked to seek forgiveness from others in situations where it will be hard for him. Unless he has hope, the counselee is not likely to do so. For him to persevere under such circumstances is vital. Sometimes counselees will fail, revert to former practices, and then fall into sin again. It is easy to give up under those conditions. So it is important for you to determine early in the first session whether or not the counselee has hope. If he does not, you must help him to hope once again (or for the first time).

What is hope? Hope in the Bible – the kind of hope that we are discussing – is not like the sort of hope that we so often talk about today. Ours today is a "hope-so" hope. We often hope against hope. In the Bible, however, "hope" refers to a certainty. It means the expectation of an event that is sure to take place. What makes it "hope" is the mere fact that it hasn't taken place yet (cf. Romans 8:24–25). But it is *certain* because God has promised it. The "blessed hope" of Titus 2:13 is certainly not a blessed hope-so! No, it is the "joyous expectation," or the "happy anticipation"[1] of the appearing of the Lord Jesus as the great God and Savior that He is.[2] That will happen. It is a certain hope.

---

1 Other possible translations that better convey the thought to modern ears.
2 Strictly speaking, according to the passage, the blessed hope is *His coming*; not *our going*.

That hope is important in the first session became apparent to me at an early point in my counseling experience. A counselee whose life was terribly entangled in bad interpersonal relationships appeared to have little hope. So I set aside the data gathering that I would normally spend time engaging in at this point to give him hope. I turned to the promises of the Scriptures (which are the source of all legitimate hope) and showed him that there was every reason to believe that God could disentangle these problem situations. Then I ended the session with prayer and got up to see the counselee to the door. When I get up, counselees also get up and we move to the door together. But he didn't. Since I felt a little foolish standing there alone, I returned to my desk chair and said, "It looks like you want to say something more." He indicated that he did. So I said, "Okay. What is it?" He reached for his wallet (I thought that he was going to try to pay me), and he pulled out a razor blade wrapped in oiled paper. Then he said, "If I hadn't gotten hope here tonight, I was going to use this on my wrists!" So, you see, you may have all sorts of interesting data at the end of the first session, but you may not have a counselee, if you don't give him hope.

I said that hope comes from the promises of God found in the Bible. Listen to Paul writing in Romans 15:13:

> Now may the God of hope fill you with every sort
> of joy and peace in believing, so that you may have
> an abundance of hope by the power of the Holy
> Spirit.

Notice he says that God is the Source of hope: as the "God of hope," He is the one from Whom all true hope flows. Other sources of hope let people down. He never does. When He calls upon us to expect or anticipate something, it is something that *will* happen. And it is through the Holy Spirit that He gives this abundant hope. How does the Holy Spirit effect hope in the believer? The answer is found earlier in the same chapter:

> Whatever was written before was written for our
> instruction, that by the endurance and the encour-

agement that the Scriptures give us we may have hope (Romans 15:4).

Clearly, it is not right to expect the Holy Spirit to "zap" hope into a counselee. As always, the Spirit works through the means that He Himself provided for the purpose – the Scriptures. In a special way, the Scriptures are *His* book. It was He Who moved the biblical authors to write them (II Peter 1:20, 21). And He uses the books that He caused them to write in achieving His purposes. Looking at these two verses, it becomes apparent that the Spirit gives hope through the Scriptures as He enlightens counselors and counselees to understand. So, counselor, in giving counselees hope, you must discover what passages of Scripture supply the promises of God that appertain to their situations. In applying these, those who trust His Word will find hope. And that hope will carry them through the hard times to God's joyous conclusions.

One passage that biblical counselors have found especially helpful in bringing hope to disheartened counselees is I Corinthians 10:13. In that passage, as I have shown in my little booklet *Christ and Your Problems* Paul makes it clear that to say "I can't" is not an option when God says that one can.[1] Too many Christians have given up, saying, "I can't do it. I can't go on. I can't take it any more, etc." In the verse God says three encouraging things:

1. You are not the first one to face trials like yours. Others have – successfully.
2. God will suit the trial to your capacities.
3. God will bring you out of the trial in His time and way.

Now those three promises – and that is what they are – when rightly understood, rightly applied, and rightly believed, will engender hope in any Christian counselee. Along with many others, use them frequently in counseling to bring hope to

---

1 Many counselors hand out this booklet to every counselee. You never can tell when there is one who claims to have hope who does not. And sometimes, even when there has been hope present, events occur between sessions that tend to discourage. The booklet can sustain them until the next session.

doubting, discouraged, and despairing counselees. The Bible is full of promises. Start collecting and memorizing them (or their locations) so that you may use them in the first session. There always are people, of course, who come brimming with hope. If you have successfully counseled others who have recommended you to them, it is likely that they will come with hope. While you will not want to set aside normal data gathering for giving hope in such cases, you will want at some point to mention the hope that God provides for them in the Bible. Again, be sure that from the outset in this first session you point to God's Word rather than yourself as the source of hope. At times, *you* will fail; *God* never will.

And in all your conversations with counselees, maintain a hopeful attitude. Counselees often are skillful in detecting whether or not *you* have hope. If you don't, stop counseling others and engage in a thorough study of biblical promises until your heart is filled with them and the impetus they will give you to counsel. No counselee needs your doubts or discouragements added to his own!

It is good to talk about God's promises in the first session – no matter what condition the counselee may be in – because at later points, when counseling gets difficult, you will want them to have understood that there is hope to be found in the Scriptures. Indeed, it is not wrong to let people know that most counseling is no snap: that there will be some tough sledding ahead, that they will need to rely upon God's promises in those times which are likely to come. Forewarned is forearmed.

Chapter Six

Agenda Adjusting

I have mentioned the need to adjust the agenda of many counselees before trying to proceed further. Until you do, when there is a need to do it, you and your counselee will be heading in different directions. Counseling will look like the man who hopped onto his horse and rode off to the East and the West at the same time. It won't be a very pretty sight!

Do some come with a proper agenda? Yes, but they are probably in the minority. Others, yes and no. By that I mean their agenda is partially correct, but even that part is wrong because it is made to be their primary (and often sole) goal.

How can you know when an agenda is proper? First, remember the PDI question "What do you want us to do about it?" The answer to that is your first and, in most cases, best clue to what a person's agenda is. If you read, "I want to get rid of the pain of this situation," you know that the agenda is probably wholly wrong. God may have brought a person into a painful situation in order to challenge, grow, and bless him. To be rid of it (at least for the present, or in the way he wishes) would be to dump God's blessing overboard. What the Lord may want in a given situation is to teach endurance (how to hang in there when the going gets tough), greater dependence on Him, or how to help others whom he could not if he were "rid of" the painful circumstance. You cannot know whether these are things that God is teaching your counselee, however, though you may throw them out as possibilities in adjusting his agenda. It may be, of course, that God does want to remove the pain. But even then, that cannot be the first objective; it must be the by-product of achieving a greater objective. What is that greater objective? In all counseling cases, the one uppermost objective that you must help a counselee etch out for himself is this: *to please God in this situation*.

The reason that I say "yes and no" in a given case is this: when a counselee's professed goal is to "get his wife back," that is a perfectly good goal under most circumstances. Nevertheless, it ought not to be the primary goal. He ought to say, "While I want my wife, I want to do what pleases God – whether my wife returns or not." Otherwise, if she doesn't return, then he probably will stop doing those things that please God, which he had been doing not as an *end*, but only as a *means* to an end. But if his goal (end) is to please God, that goal can be achieved whether or not his wife returns. If she returns, he will be a better husband for having done those things that God wanted. If she doesn't return, he will be in better shape to handle that because he has done those things that please God. And most of all, he will have pleased God – which is the chief end of life. By looking at this example, it should be clear to you that pleasing God must always be the primary goal. When the end is right, the side effects (by-products) will also fall in line in time.

There have been times when a husband and wife have come for counseling and the two say something like this:

Wife: "I'm about to leave him. I can't stand things like they are anymore!"

Husband: "Awww, she exaggerates things. There isn't much of a problem at all."

What do you do when their descriptions of the problem – and thus their secondary objectives in counseling – are so very far apart? You can always find something in the very dissonance itself to set forth as a problem: "Well, one thing is certain – you two don't communicate very well if your description of the problem is that different! Obviously, we must work on communication. But, let's consider another thing: God says in I Peter 3:7:

> Husbands, likewise live with your wives in an understanding way, showing respect for the woman as you would for a fragile vase, and as joint heirs of the grace of life, so that your prayers may not be interrupted.

41

According to Peter, until you get your communication with your wife on a level of understanding, you cannot expect your communication with God to work out either. It is like when a teenager wants the keys to the family car but has not sought forgiveness from his sister; he isn't likely to get them. The father is likely to say instead, "Don't ask me for anything until you've gotten that matter with your sister straightened out." *There is something that comes first.*[1] That is what you are looking for in many cases – what God says comes first.

But then there are also cases where the counselee wants something plainly wrong or, at least, very questionable. Naturally, you will show him from the Scriptures what is wrong with his goal. He may not marry that unbeliever, even though he says that he "loves" her. In I Corinthians 7:39 it is clear that a believer is to "marry only in the Lord." If he puts her before the Lord, when he knows God's clear command, he is coveting her, and that is idolatry (Colossians 3:5); he has put her acquisition before God's commandment. You will point this out in a kindly but explicit way.

On the other hand, if an action is very questionable, you must be prepared to explain the *holding principle* found in Romans 14:23, "whatever isn't done in faith is sin." That means that if one does something that he thinks *might* be sin (even if it isn't) he has sinned. "How is that?" you ask. In this way: while the action itself was not wrong, the attitude in which the counselee did it was. He was willing to do something that he thought might be wrong in God's sight. That was a sinful attitude. So, until he is convinced from the Bible that God considers an act righteous, he may not move ahead; he must put the act on hold indefinitely. If, in time, he discovers that it would be sin, he must disregard it completely. If, in time, he discovers that it would not be sin to do it, he may then go forward with the

---

1 Cf. Matthew 6:14–15, where the same dynamic is at work. Clearly, doing what God requires first is essential to some other end that one might have in view. And it must not be done as a means to that end. It must be done to please Him.

action. In either case, the important thing is to honor God in one's attitudes and actions.

Negotiating and/or adjusting agendas is an important matter. You may discover that your agenda (hopefully, the same as God's) and that of your counselee are far apart. I spoke to a Christian school administrator who was telling me about the goals that teachers and students had in mind for their education. They gave a stack of ten items to both students and teachers and asked them to pile them up in the order of importance. They included such things as glorifying God, getting a good job upon graduation, making a large salary, serving others, and the like. It was revealing that while the majority of the students put such things as a large salary and a good job at the top of the list, while placing glorifying God at the bottom, the teachers reversed the items in the pile. That study of agendas made it clear that it would take some work to negotiate and adjust the objectives of the students in that system. Otherwise, teacher and student would be shooting past one another. The same is true in counseling.

If a counselee refuses to change his agenda when he realizes that God requires the change, it will be useless to continue with counseling. The problem has shifted from whatever the presenting problem may have been to, "What sort of agenda should a counselee have when he enters counseling?" If he is willing to counsel about this, you may continue. If he is unwilling, you must stop until he is willing to do so, or has come to a proper biblical agenda on his own. Sometimes counselors are so accommodating to their counselees that they will allow them – rather than God – to set their agendas. That is a mistake. Indeed, it must always be the counselor's agenda to require God's agenda. If this is not your agenda, you will be helping counselees go in the wrong direction, confirming them in sinful and unbiblical ways. Don't do it!

"What if a counselee says that his agenda is God's just to get my help – when it really isn't? He doesn't mean it in his heart." It is not your task to try to determine what is in another's heart. The Scripture says, "Man looks on the outward appearance, but the Lord looks at the heart" (I Samuel 16:7, NASB) and the title "the Heart-Newer" is given to God, not to a man (Acts 1:24); in contrast to others, of Jesus it was said that "He knew what was in human beings" (John 2:25).[1] It is the task of the counselor to evaluate what the counselee does and says. If the counselee lies, that will become apparent in time as homework assignments will be built on what he says and does. He will not be able to accomplish these if he has been giving you false data. Then will be the time to inquire into whether the data he has provided are true or false. Until you have tangible evidence to doubt what he says, you must "believe all things, hope all things" in love (I Corinthians 13:7).

It is possible that the counselee gave you false information unintentionally. He may not be lying after all. He may simply be mistaken or misinformed. Then, you will spend some time helping him to determine how to sift true from false data when it turns out that the responsibility was his for not checking the information adequately. But this is not something you will do during the first session. It will come later on.

Now, since you cannot read another's heart (it is hard enough to read your own), what you can do is warn the counselee that he must give you true data so far as he understands them. If he isn't sure, then urge him to say so. If he is, let him say that too. But lies, or half-truths (which are usually lies, too) only slow down the process of counseling and displease God. These facts should be made known from the outset. There is usually an opportunity to tell this to the counselee in the first session. Instead of waiting to catch him in a lie, it is better to

---

1 In the two chapters following (John 3, John 4) we see how He knew what was in the hearts of Nicodemus and of the woman at the well. Too often counselors today seem to think that they can know another's heart. They cannot; that is God's prerogative, and His alone. They must refrain from every attempt to encroach on His domain. There is often a kind of talk in some nouthetic counseling circles about "idols of the heart" that seems quite suspicious. In Ezekiel 14, where this expression occurs, it is not the idols that one invents (like idols of lust, of money, etc.) but the idols that God had taken them away

warn ahead of time. Tell him that you want to hear the truth, the whole truth (that he knows), and no shading of the truth.

Remind your counselee that what he does and says is taking place in the presence of God. Here is another opportunity to develop the proper atmosphere. Let him know that though he may color the truth in ways that seem more acceptable to you, God sees right through the false shades with which he may try to paint over it. Tell him that in God's sight all is open and plain (Hebrews 4:12–13), that He will take action that accords with the truth, rather than with some false representation of it. You can say all of this in the first session *as a matter of routine*, not as though you suspect him of lying. Clearly, if you say it early in the session, before you have much data at all, he will know that you are not charging him with falsehood. That is the opportune time to do so. If in sessions later on he is caught in a lie, then you can refer back to this warning that you gave him at first. It will not come out of the sky as a thunderbolt but, rather, as a reminder. So agendas must not only be proper, biblical agendas in reference to the goals that one sets for counseling, they must be based on truth and openness. Trimming the sharp edge off the truth or concealing essential material is taboo.

Let me stress that last point too. In talking about the matter of truthfully revealing the situation, even though it may put your counselee in a bad light, be careful to emphasize that the "whole" truth (as much of it as he knows) ought to be set forth. Naturally, not every jot and tittle must be given, but all that is necessary to a correct understanding of the situation should be forthcoming. There are those who will tell you half of the truth when the other half throws quite a different light on an event.

---

from through the exile. Yet even though He had removed them from this idolatry in order to cleanse them from it, they had carried those very same idols into exile in their hearts. This idea of "idols of lust, idols of sex," etc., as if a counselor could discern that these are in one's heart, sounds suspiciously like the "demons of lust," etc. that others postulate. There is possible danger here that must be avoided. Since the Bible never uses such a construct, we ought not do so. When man looks on the outward appearance, he judges actions and words; God alone judges the heart.

"He hit me! He hit me in the face!" she said. "Yes, she was running around screaming hysterically, beating herself on her head. I thought she'd damage herself seriously, so I did what they do on TV, I slapped her in order to bring her to her senses." The two stories, taken together, tell a different story than the one story given alone does. The husband's solution to the problem at hand might not have been the wisest one, but his expressed motive was not that bad after all. The whole truth usually makes a difference.

To set up God's agenda in the first session, if at all possible, is an important task. It is one that a counselor avoids at his own and at the counselee's peril. If you don't get any farther than setting it up properly, if it takes the lion's share of the session to do so, then do it. Forget other matters; they won't matter in the long run anyway if your agenda and that of the counselee(s) differ.

Chapter Seven
Counselees You Will Meet

There are counselees of every kind. Just when you think that you have met them all, a counselee of a sort that you have never encountered before will arrive at your office. That means that in this chapter I can no more cover all of the types of counselees than I could explain all of the problems that they might have. I shall, however, mention some of the more common counselee problems with which you may have to deal, and just a bit of what you can do initially in helping them to relate to people.

The thought that some initial biblical direction may be given to a counselee in the very first session is foreign to many counselors. They think that you must spend inordinate amounts of time dredging out the hidden causes of a counselee's problems. Ordinarily, no such thing is true. In fact, in most cases if he will, the counselee himself can fairly accurately tell you what his problem is. When he can't, or when he only half tells, other obvious signs and data elicited may alert you to the facts.

Initial direction, whenever possible, should be given to the counselee for at least three reasons:

1. You want him to know that the Bible has answers to life's problems; that it is a practical Book. Many Christians use their Bibles as though they were for reading purposes only. They must be taught that the Bible relates directly to their everyday lives, and that in it God's perfect directions for living may be found.

2. You want to give him some indication – if only a glimpse – of where counseling is going in future sessions. Even the homework that you give will be calculated to effect this result.

3. You want him to recognize that you will not waste time or allow him to do so. While you will not rush ahead to hasty judgments (you will always qualify any initial directions that you

give him),[1] on the other hand, you will make it clear that you expect things to happen – and to happen rather quickly. So, then, what sort of counselees are you likely to meet?

Complaining, Whining Grumblers

Any one of or all of these responses will be present from the outset. Singly, these approaches to life and in relation to others are bad; in combination, they are horrendous. People like this are hard to be around. They think primarily of themselves. You may wish they wouldn't come for counseling, but that isn't how it is. In counseling offices, they abound.

According to this type of counselee, it is always the other person's fault. People like this occasionally may concede that they "may have" done something wrong, "but compared to what so-and-so did, well..." They, of all people, have been put upon; nobody has ever had to endure so much before.[2] They will find fault with their church, the preacher, you, your counseling (yes, possibly even in the first session![3]), their spouses, other friends – you name it! "Why?" is a question often found on their lips, but they really aren't looking for answers; they just want to complain. Their greatest pleasure is in finding fault.

---

1 For instance, you will say such things as, "Now, if I am anywhere near the truth in understanding your problem, I want you to know that God has spoken most clearly about how to deal with it. In Ephesians 4 he has given us some basic help about how to overcome anger..." Moreover, you will also say such things as, "I recognize that this may not be your only problem. As we go along, we may uncover others. But for now..." These qualifiers, tacked on to an *initial* assessment, and some *initial* directions as to how God wants the counselee to solve the problem, in most cases, should not only accomplish the three things noted above; they should also give hope. Many counselees have been in counseling sessions before where the counselor did nothing but listen. To indicate that there is a direction to go, and that you intend to help the counselee take it, is to them remarkable. At this point, I have had counselees say such things as, "You mean we're actually going to *do* something about the problem?" while uttering a sigh of relief.

2 Again, remember the usefulness of I Corinthians 10:13, especially the first promise.

3 No matter what you do, there will be something wrong with it.

Obviously, whether there is some other problem or not, they do have a problem with grumbling. And you must deal with it, no matter what other problems they may present. If you don't, you will get nowhere in counseling because, instead of cooperation, you will find yourself constantly having to handle complaints. So take them on in the first session. You might refer to I Corinthians 10, in which Paul deals directly with the subject of grumbling. He mentions how the complaints of the Israelites in the wilderness led to the disastrous results mentioned in verse 5. Read verses 1 through 13 to your counselee, and say, "It is important for us to deal with the problems mentioned in these verses if we are going to get anywhere with your other counseling problems."

Show counselees how God hates grumbling and how He dealt with it. Observe, since God is sovereign, He sends everything that comes into our lives for our good (Romans 8:28–29), among other things, to make us more like Christ. That means that grumbling of all forms is grumbling against God! Making that point ought to be somewhat sobering. Tell your counselee that you know that this is probably a sinful habit and that it may take a while to develop new habits in place of these old ones, but that if he is willing, you can help him do so (you might refer in passing to the put off/put on dynamic in Ephesians 4). But you will countenance no more grumbling in the process. Then he can become a more cheerful person that others will appreciate.

Those Who Are Angry

The grumbler may also be angry. Others, however, may save all their energy for fighting – verbally or otherwise. They are angry and they will let you know it. Either their rage will be vented in ways that are unmistakable, or they will indicate by their acidic vocabulary and their descriptions of others with whom they are angry that down inside they are furious. The anger may be vented or muffled, but it can hardly be hidden. Anger is an emotion that is designed to tear apart, to destroy. It seeks opportunities to do so in one way or another.

In giving your angry counselee some indication of how you will help him deal with his anger, you will probably want to read him some of the material relating to anger in Ephesians 4. Other passages might eventually be brought to bear upon his problem, as sessions continue, but the only other one likely to come into the discussion in the initial session is Proverbs 29:11 (NIV), where the writer says that it is a "fool" who "gives full vent to his anger." Clearly, acting that way is foolishness, something for which no one wants to be known. Help your counselee see that he can overcome anger by doing as Paul directs in Ephesians 4 neither by internalizing his anger nor by giving vent to it, but by releasing it under control at the problem rather than at persons. There is a lot of energy in anger. That energy should be put to good use. It will be when directed toward the problem with a view toward solving it: "I simply *will not* let up until this problem is solved!!!"

The Depressed

Frequently, but not always, combined with other problems (marital difficulties, the loss of a job, etc.) those whose problem is depression will appear in a steady stream. Their problem, you may initially observe, is an old one, but so is God's solution. Turning to II Corinthians 4, where Paul says that he would not "give up" (CCNT) in spite of his many afflictions (see chapters 6, 11), you may show how there is another way to respond to life's trials. Because of his love and gratitude to God, Paul soldiered on: "Therefore, since we have this service to perform as the result of mercy, we don't give up" (v. 1).

How did he do it? He refused to follow his feelings – which must have taunted him, saying, "What's the use?" as they do to your counselee – but went on doing his responsibilities before God. In faithfully serving Him he found the answer: he never despaired (vv. 8–9). In a sense, depression is the cowardly way out. And the modern method of dealing with it through medicine matches and encourages that weakening approach to life's problems. The biblical way is to go on *in spite of feelings;* and when one does, he will not become depressed. Similarly, the way out of depression (which can be rapid and lasting) is to pitch in, and once again assume those responsibilities that have been abandoned. That will bring about the desired change of mood. But the counselee should not merely seek to feel better. Rather, first and foremost, he should desire to assume his responsibilities for God's glory.

A depressed person (whose catchword is "can't") is useless in the kingdom of God. He has "given up." He needs to hear the words of I Corinthians 15:58. Serving God is never in vain; and we can always accomplish what He requires of us if we avail ourselves of His wisdom and strength. The believer has a place in Christ's church. He is needed. He must not shirk his responsibility there (Galatians 6:5) or to his family and employer. Nor need he do so. Giving up isn't something that one ever needs to do when he knows Jesus Christ as Savior. Let your depressed counselee know that this condition may be turned around even this week if he is willing to have it happen. Find out what he has been failing to do – in the various areas of his life – and draw up a plan for him to get to work on at least some of them right away. The lower the pile of work gets, the higher his spirits will rise!

The Fearful

Fear can be a powerful emotion. It can drive people to fight, to flee, or to freeze. The biblical response to fear is to *face* it. And a believer in Jesus Christ can do so. The thousands of martyrs who went to their deaths rather than deny their Lord found that He was able to sustain them in the face of terrifying opponents. How was that so? They understood and believed Jesus' words in Matthew 14:26–33.

> The disciples saw Him walking on the sea and were terrified and said, "It is a ghost!" And they screamed from fear. But immediately He spoke to them, saying, "Have courage; it is I. Don't be afraid." In response, Peter said, "Lord, if it is You, let me come to You on the water." And He said,

"Come." So Peter got down from the ship and walked on the water toward Jesus. But when he looked at the wind, he was afraid, and beginning to sink he shouted, "Lord, save me!" Immediately Jesus stretched out His hand, took hold of him and said to him, "Little-faith, why did you doubt?" And when they climbed up into the boat, the wind stopped blowing. So those who were in the boat worshiped Him, saying, "Truly You are God's Son."

It is not enough to profess faith in Christ in times of danger. That faith must enable the Christian to withstand the enemy – whomever he may be. When one finds himself in the presence of danger, it is time to remember his Lord and His power to enable him to endure or escape in an honorable, biblical way. The open secret, of course, is found in these verses: one must fear God more than one fears man. That is the ultimate answer to fear that you will offer to the counselee. In addition to the Matthew 14 passage, you might also mention John's important words, "There is no fear in love; rather, love that has attained its goal throws fear out" (I John 4:18). When one loves God and others more than himself, he will not fear. Fear *is* a powerful emotion; but love is more powerful. One does as God commands out of love, *regardless of the consequences.*

Those Who Are Grieving

Grief, as Paul makes clear in I Thessalonians 4:13 and following, is proper. But grief apart from the Christian hope is sinful. Christians need not grieve as does the world because they know the assured facts of life and death. They know the future and what it holds for them and their loved ones. The facts in that closing paragraph of I Thessalonians 4 are enough to make the difference between believing grief and unbelieving grief. The hope of the resurrection is a marvelous expectation to which every believer must cling.

Grieving over a long period of time is wrong. A reasonable amount of time is understandable, but debilitating grief over months and months – even years – becomes sinful. The counselor must help persons who have extended their grief in this manner to take their place once again in the ranks of those who are faithfully serving their Lord. The problem here is that they have become self-centered and may want to prolong the pity and concern that others have shown them at the time of death. Instead of rebounding in time, they have attempted to drag out the special love and care extended to them at the time of death. They also may become angry when people no longer show the same concern after the funeral flowers have died. Help such persons to turn the spotlight off themselves and on Christ and others in His church. Help them to see that God has left them here for a purpose. Help them to find that purpose and "get with it."

The Guilty

Notice, we are not talking about those who have "guilt feelings," or "false guilt." The psychologists have avoided dealing with true guilt in favor of these other constructions. There is no false guilt. Guilt is real. When one is concerned that he may have committed a guilty act (which in fact is not sinful), he is guilty (truly so) for having acted as he did when he thought (even if wrongly) that what he was doing was sin. His attitude toward God was sinful.

Guilt feelings are the concern of many counselors – i.e., how to eliminate them. Some say (in effect) to weaken the conscience (lower the standards); others try to eliminate bad feelings by means of medication or denying the guilt of an act altogether. Neither is the answer. The biblical way to deal with guilt is to confess the sin and forsake it (Proverbs 28:13).

Repentance is the answer. Repentance (which may be necessary in the first session for most of your counselees) consists of two things: "Changing one's mind; changing his actions." In Isaiah 55:6–9, God makes it clear that sinful man's thoughts and ways are not His thoughts and ways. God isn't going to change His thinking or His ways; so man must. That is repentance. The

New Testament word speaks of the change of mind (*metanoieo* = "to rethink") and the Old Testament word refers to change of action (*shuv* = "to turn around and go the opposite way"). So repentance is a change of mind that leads to a change of direction.

To deny guilt, or to attempt to eliminate it altogether, is cruel, as Karl Menninger demonstrated in his book *Whatever Became of Sin?* As he says, there are many unforgiven people whose sins are being called crimes or sicknesses rather than sin. You do not forgive crime or sickness; you only forgive sin. They need forgiveness but will never receive it until they come to grips with their sin and seek the forgiveness of God and of others. Menninger's solution is wrong because it isn't biblical. But his analysis of the problem is correct.

Help counselees to see that sin is against God first of all, even when others have been wronged. It is disobedience to His commandments. If God says to do something and a person does not – that's sin. If He forbids something, and the person does it anyway – that's also sin. To call sin "sin" is the kindest thing to do. Why? Because calling it something else takes away hope. Christ came to die for *sinners*; He didn't come to die for sickness or some genetic problem. There is all the hope that one might wish in Christ to overcome sin. So always speak in terms of sin to the guilty person. It is a word that he seldom hears, but the fact is that he is involved in it and needs to be forgiven of it. You may have to discuss the various aspects of forgiveness with him, so you must understand thoroughly the ins and the outs of forgiveness. I have written extensively on the subject in my book *From Forgiven to Forgiving* (q.v.).

The Proud

Ordinarily, people don't come for counsel regarding their pride. They use all sorts of other terms when describing it – terms that mask the reality to them as well as to those to whom they speak. For instance, what is a "shy" person? It is a person who is afraid to be embarrassed. He is proud. Should he fail at something, should others laugh at him, talk about him behind his back – well, that would devastate him. Why? Because he thinks he deserves better. He is too proud to have to go through the awkward and embarrassing stages of learning how to play an instrument, learning to skate, and so on. So, with a sour grapes attitude, he downgrades what he will not learn to do.

Take another manifestation of pride: "hurt feelings." Of course, the expression is a faulty description of the facts; feelings don't get hurt! What does? The person does. In many cases, he sticks his foot out and then when someone treads on it, he begins to cry and complain about their treatment of him. Even when he doesn't stick his foot out, if someone wrongs him (or he thinks that someone has), his sense of self-importance is so large that either he will not ignore the slight (or other wrong) and go about his business, or he will not confront the person to settle the problem biblically. His attitude is "Let him come to me. He did it!"

Such persons need to have their "self-esteem" lowered – not raised, as the psychologists think. They need a large dose of Romans 12:3 in combination with Luke 17:3. At times, a dash of Matthew 18:15 and following, might not hurt. But by all means, such counselees must be shown how pride is at the heart of their problem: "I am too important to be treated this way!" In light of the problem, be sure to introduce the warning of Proverbs 16:18 into the mix, "Pride goes before destruction" (NIV).

Persons Who Behave Bizarrely

From time to time persons exhibiting bizarre behavior may come for counseling. If there is any reason to suspect neurological problems, by all means advise a medical checkup. But much (perhaps most) bizarre behavior does not stem from organic problems. It is true that there could be a tumor on the brain or some other organic cause, but consider additional causes as well. Drug-induced behavior (check this out thoroughly at the outset) may be at the bottom of the problem. Chemicals involuntarily ingested at one's place of work could be the difficulty. Sleep loss, which in some persons can lead to every effect of LSD, is very common. See if the person has been missing sleep (if he is harming his body in this way, urge him to take a sleep binge, then find out what he has been losing sleep over). Pretense in order to excuse some wrong behavior ("Oh, John couldn't help it. You know how he is...") or in order to obtain something by it. Don't hesitate to take on such cases. More often than not, you will find that you can help.

Couples with Marital Problems

Plainly, these will be very common. In my book *Solving Marriage Problems* I have explored most of the essential matters with which you ought to be concerned. Perhaps here I ought only to deal with the various strains of problems that you will find yourself encountering. These strains may be single, or as is more often the case, tangled with one another:

1. *Communication problems.* If not the fundamental problem, communication breakdown will often result from failure to deal biblically with others. The communication dilemma is this: counselees need to be able to communicate to deal with the communication problem. You, therefore, are important in helping them learn how to do so.

2. *Sexual problems.* Usually, these problems are not organic, but relational. What happens when a couple crawls under the sheets at night often is not as important as what has happened after crawling out from under them in the morning. It is the daily, unresolved difficulties that they carry to bed at night that are the culprits. So, unless in the unlikely event that there is failure in proper use of sexual technique, investigate the non-sexual relationship of the husband and the wife.

Of course, there are serious problems in the understanding of sexual relationships that can only be corrected by an understanding and application of the principles in I Corinthians 7. There the institution of foreplay is considered mutual, the satisfaction of one's wife or husband comes before his or her own, the regularity of sexual relations is stressed, etc. See *The Christian Counselor's Manual* for details. Complaints may stem from the use of pornography in video, TV, or the internet. Check this out carefully to be sure that complication is not present. Physical adultery or adultery of the heart may be involved. You also will want to check out these possibilities.

3. *Money problems.* You may need to help married couples set up a budget, to learn to communicate more fully with one another about spending decisions, to teach them how to keep records (if you have an accountant in the church who will help, enlist him), and matters of this sort.

There may be cheating on income tax records, pilfering at work or some other petty theft, or, for that matter, grand theft or embezzlement. These things are not unknown. Questions about when to bring the law into the picture in the case of crimes, helping counselees restore stolen property or funds, and the like may emerge. You must be ready to face these hard situations squarely. When you are not sure about what to do, you may need to admit it and search for the information that you need. Try to befriend a Christian lawyer from whom you can obtain advice about legal questions.

The love of money can lead to every sort of abuse. Surely you will want to bring the principles found in I Timothy 6:5–11; 17[1]–19 to bear upon money problems. If theft has occurred, then Ephesians 4:28 will be apropos.

4. *Child-rearing conflicts.* When things go wrong, there is a tendency for one spouse to blame the other rather than working together to resolve the problems. This only complicates matters, a development which a rebellious child is likely to exploit to the fullest. Often you will need to bring the child in for counseling – especially if he is old enough to understand. And you want to be sure that you don't talk negatively behind his back. Let him in on the conversation so that everyone knows that everyone knows what everyone knows. Then there can be no misunderstandings growing out of lack of knowledge. You will need to get commitments all around that all concerned require of each other.

---

1 In accordance with verse 17, it may be necessary for you to set up a rich man's Bible study.

Demanding Persons

It is amazing how people who have lived with problems for months – or years – suddenly demand that you settle their difficulties overnight. Or they will want to take inordinate amounts of your time outside the counseling room talking over the phone, sending letters or e-mail, and so on. Make it clear to them that only a certain amount of time is available, and that there are other persons whom you are helping as well as them. When they want to speak to you on the phone about counseling matters, have the secretary refuse (politely) and tell them to "write it down and bring it to the next counseling session." Tell them that you cannot do good counseling on the phone; that their lives are too important to give short shrift to their problems – as you would have to do "on the fly." Don't lose control of the counseling relationship in or outside the sessions themselves. Start teaching inconsiderate counselees – as most demanding counselees turn out to be – some consideration of you and your time, as well as that of others.

There are persons with other counseling problems, but these I have mentioned will constitute the bulk of your counseling load. Yet, be ready for anything. Most of the verses mentioned, along with the initial responses suggested, will help you to meet other problems head-on as well. Become acquainted with these and add others to your list for use in the first session. When you get into later sessions, you will expound on these and additional verses in more depth where necessary. But in the first session, remember, you are giving initial, helpful indications of counseling will go. That is the key thing, as well as getti counselee started on the biblical solutions to his problems.

Chapter Eight
Data Gathering

I am not going to replicate the in-depth material on this subject that is found in my book *The Christian Counselor's Manual.* Instead, I shall simply suggest certain additional aspects of the matter that, in conjunction with the material already given in the *Manual,* should enhance your ability to gather relevant and important data from counselees.

First, your attitude. I have reminded you elsewhere that you are not a Freudian. You believe that although people are sinful and may fail, they often try to give you true data. Freudians do not believe this. Because of their fundamental doctrine of man (he is driven by unconscious, irrational desires that he rationalizes to himself and to others), Freudians believe the counselee will always tell a false story. In contrast, while Christian counselors recognize that sinners lie, distort, and give incomplete stories, counselors should nevertheless take the word of another Christian as substantially true, unless the facts later on demonstrate it to be inaccurate or untrue. The Christian counselor therefore begins with a loving attitude toward the counselee (love "believes all things," I Cor. 13:7). He is not antagonistic, as the Freudian inevitably is, but friendly to the counselee.[1] He will search for facts, not for devious motives behind them. Of course, a counselee may have distorted facts (intentionally, or unintentionally), and in later sessions that must be dealt with. But, when asked properly, most counselees will attempt to give the counselor the data he needs. So the wise counselor will work

---

1 Some would dispute the charge that the Freudian is antagonistic. I believe he is, since beginning with the idea that a counselee is always falsifying truth (albeit unknowingly) places the counselor in an antagonistic position to the counselee. He must always be on his guard lest he take what the counselee says to be true. He must always question the counselee's stated motives and positions. His whole orientation is antagonistic, whether his feelings are or not – and too often they will be!

diligently to obtain all relevant data, scraping his counselee's memory clear to the bottom.

Your attitude, then, will be that of one Christian brother helping another. It will be friendly and helpful, not charged with suspicion. Always remember Galatians 6:1–2, in which you are exhorted to have an attitude of "meekness." You must therefore avoid any sort of assumed superiority. And don't fail to notice that in the same passage Paul warns against temptations that counseling may occasion. In view of the many counselors who have fallen into sexual sin, in particular, that warning is timely.

Remember, before the first session begins, you already have much information from the Bible and from the PDI. From Scripture, you know that, as a believer, your counselee is a forgiven sinner. You also know that he is in the process of being sanctified; he has not reached perfection. So he is capable of committing most sins. An experienced counselor is rarely shocked at anything he hears.

You know, however, that since the Spirit dwells within him, a Christian counselee can understand the Bible and he can actually do what it directs. In other words, you know that he has the resources to solve any and all problems about which the Bible speaks. That is an enormous advantage that you have, as a Christian working with a Christian. The non-Christian counselor doesn't have a clue about the counselee's basic problem – sin. Therefore, he adopts one or more of the current views about what man's problem is (environment, poor conditioning, lack of understanding, faulty education, and so on). You have, as your presupposition, the broadest category of all to pursue: sin. Sin has led to all other subsequent, secondary problems. Because other counselors postulate that one or more of these secondary causes is primary, they distort reality. Usually, they even narrow their focus to but one of these secondary factors. You do not have to limit your thinking to the narrow views of human theorists.

Of course, there are problems in one's past education. Certainly, he has not been trained in his home as he ought to have been. Naturally, he has not had the very best environment. But why? Because of *sin,* which has led to all of these and to other defects. And you know that, because of the sinful nature with which he was born, your counselee has developed sinful attitudes, desires, and patterns of behavior. You know, then, that you will have to gather information about all of these things. That is why you must become an inveterate data-gatherer. That is why you will concern yourself with extensive as well as intensive data gathering. And in Proverbs 18:17 you are warned not to act on the basis of the insufficient, often one-sided information for which many settle.

So as a Christian who has studied what God says about people in general and in particular, you are at an advantage over the non-Christian counselor. You start out before you even talk to the counselee with a great deal of knowledge about him. Of course, if you are his pastor or elder, you will know even more about him before he enters counseling.[1]

On top of these things, you will gather and organize[2] all of the information that the PDI elicits. This, as I have indicated, is fairly extensive. Not only does it provide information to which you may need to refer as sessions proceed, it also is designed to focus on those matters that you want to know almost from the outset. Don't be like some counselors who have counselees fill out the PDI but then rarely or never refer to it again. It is a tool that you can hardly do without in most circumstances. Use it – to the fullest!

It is in the first session that data-gathering should *begin.* Normally, it will take more than one session to cull all the facts that you want. Indeed, one of the most important first session homework assignments you will give – and you will give assignments frequently – is for the counselee to work during the week on gathering additional data that he will bring back in written form for the next session. Having the counselee do that sort of work shortens the amount of time that you will spend in

---

1 A major reason for counseling under the aegis of one's church.
2 Something you should do following sessions, comparing data gathered in different ways.

counseling. After all, it is he who has lived the life experiences which you are considering, not you. Why, then, should you have to think up questions to ask him about further data when he already knows all about them? What you want to do is to *direct* his investigation for the next week into certain areas. Then set him to work collecting the details that you need.

Now, data gathering should never be done out of mere curiosity. Some counselors have been known to gather data for such purposes. For instance, there are those who, out of prurient motives, gather detailed sexual material in order to "get their kicks." Not only is this reprehensible for a Christian to do, but also on the simple, practical level, it does not help in counseling.[1] If a counselee of the opposite sex attempts to get into areas that are questionable, stop data gathering in that area and turn to another "safer" area. Moreover, when you must gather general sexual data, even then be sure that you keep the discussion on a "clinical" level. Use terms that come from the books, not from the back alleys. There are not many situations in which sexual details of any sort are needed. Be sure that you keep the discussion, therefore, on the highest and most general level possible. And remember, whenever counseling a woman, a pastor should have an elder or deacon present with him to avoid any false charges or temptations.

In data gathering, you will find that some counselees want to go over the same material again and again. You must make it clear that you already have taken notes on this, so the matter will not be omitted in later counseling, and that for the present it is important to get on to other matters. Counselees who will not leave a subject either so badly want to deal with the problem or they want to keep you away from some other one. Regardless of the reason, don't allow them to "take over" the process of data gathering by continuing to focus on only one area. If necessary, you may have to say something like this: "Since you seem to think that there is material about this subject that is of such

---

1 Take it as a counseling principle: whatever is wrong biblically is harmful to counseling.

importance, this week you may want to write out any additional facts that occur to you and bring them in at the next session." In this way, you can both dispose of the subject for the moment so that you can get on to other things and satisfy the person who is afraid that you are minimizing it.

If the counselee is anxious to avoid some other area, he will probably try the same technique with the next "safe" area that you take up. After a while, you will catch on to his ploy. It will usually be accompanied by facial or other bodily data (halo data) that becomes evident every time you approach a particular area. He will shift his seating position, grimace, look away, glance at his watch, or something of the sort. Be observant and listen carefully to what is said. Data gathering of this visual sort can be very helpful in reaching key areas.

Listen for emphases in how a person speaks. He may speak of his *"dear* wife" in tones or other ways that belie the very phrase itself. Listen too to the vocabulary that he uses. Is it the vocabulary of exaggeration, self-pity, anger, frustration, fear – or something else? Because nervousness leads to muscle tightening, one's voice rises when he is especially tense. His vocal folds, like strings on a violin, when tightened emit sounds at a higher pitch. If he tenses up and his voice rises when discussing a matter, that *may* be because you are striking pay dirt. Probe around more whenever you think that you are about to uncover a valuable vein of ore.

When you gather data, think of yourself in the counselee's place and do unto him as you would have him do unto you. There are those who gather data as if they were carrying on an interrogation down at the local precinct. You are neither a detective nor a policeman. Remember that. You are a Christian brother, as I said, who happens to be in a position to help another brother. You have no reason to browbeat him. Your attitude always ought to be kindly and helpful. And *your* vocabulary should say that you care.

Remember, when data gathering do not ask questions that begin with the word "why." To ask "what?" will get you much more information. "What" questions followed by "when, where and which" questions are the best for your purposes. And be sure to let further questions grow out of previous answers – much the way you do in ordinary conversation. But in conversation you ordinarily shelve some follow-up questions that occur to you because they are too personal or direct for polite conversation.[1] These questions may be the very best ones in counseling. When they come to mind consider asking them. You are not in mere conversation; you are counseling. The counselee has asked you to become more personal. But remember, don't ask those personal questions that have little or nothing to do with the problem at hand merely out of curiosity.

So, in data gathering, get all the significant data that you need, nothing more, and in a manner that the counselee can interpret only as helpful. But also remember, you don't have to get it all in this session. You are only *beginning*.

---

1 For instance, "I wonder if he is giving me the *whole* story?"

Chapter Nine
Initial Homework

Giving homework – work to do between weekly sessions – speeds up counseling, takes it out of the artificial setting of the counseling room into the arena where life is lived, and keeps the counselee from becoming dependent on the counselor. All three of these important factors are essential to biblical counseling.

When James spoke of showing one's faith by his works, he was saying that it is not enough to have good intentions,[1] to know what one ought to do[2] or to be able to articulate God's will.[3] Indeed, though all of those things are important, they are not enough. Faith must lead to works. Those who stress "grace" to the exclusion of works are mistaken. Grace ultimately leads to works. Paul said, "we are His handiwork, created in Christ Jesus for good works" (Ephesians 2:10). Notice, doing works is the purpose for which God created us. It is always wrong to take part of what God says to the exclusion of another part. Since works do not save, many fear all talk of works, labeling such "legalism." But that is quite wrong. If expecting grace-engendered good works from believers is legalistic, then God is the supreme Legalist! He not only demands works ("If you love Me, keep My commandments,"[4] John 14:15) but, as Paul says, He created us for the very purpose of living out our salvation in grace-works for His glory. And those good works which He expects are precisely those that He Himself "prepared before-

---

1 Some stress the importance of the heart in a biblically unbalanced way. Heart commitment should always lead to newness of life.

2 Knowledge is essential also, but it is no substitute for action.

3 Some are all talk and no action; glibness is not the same as accomplishment.

4 In Scripture, love is "shown" by works ("God so loved…that He *gave*"); the two are only antithetical when set against each other as ways of salvation. One becomes righteous by faith (not works), but demonstrates that faith in works that stem from the new birth.

hand"[1] so that we "might walk in them" (Ephesians 2:10[b]). The counselor, then, expects to see change in the form of works. That is one reason he gives home*work*.[2]

Now, what is homework all about? It is the counselee's opportunity to follow through on the commitments that he makes in the counseling sessions. It is the outworking of the principles that he adopts by faith and in his heart determines to do for God's glory. It is the place where he learns how to apply truth (cf. Titus 1:1).[3] It is how he deals with his former sin in relation to others and, instead, now does righteousness.

The counselee will fail, fall, often become bruised in the process – just as the novice ice skater does when he takes up skating. But he will persevere by grace until he learns to overcome former sinful habit patterns and in their place establish new, righteous ones. Counselors will tell counselees these things and help them get over the awkward stage so that their growth becomes apparent to them and to others, and until they are able to "walk" in God's ways without the counselor's support.

Homework ought to be given at every session. That includes the first. In the first session the counselor establishes his methodology. If he waits until several sessions later to begin giving homework, he will have already established a policy of non-homework which he must later break! That is foolish. Moreover, Jesus often told His counselees to do things on the very first encounter He had with them. You are not Jesus, but you are ministering His Word. Jesus seemed to think that *some* change in the counselee could take place right away; so should you.

The change for which you call or the homework that you give should not be too great at the outset. But it should be adapted to the situation and to the counselee himself. For

---

1 Why would God determine beforehand what good works we should do if they were not of importance to Him? Indeed, here Paul says that He prepared them *so that* we might walk in them.
2 Call it "projects" for school children!
3 Truth has as its goal godly living, not mere possession of knowledge.

instance, often in a first session I will give this assignment to a couple: "Write out a *small* list of one hundred or more ways[1] in which you are displeasing God as a person, as a husband (or wife) and as a father (or mother). Draw a line under what you have written and hand it to your spouse to add any items he or she thinks were omitted." That sort of assignment is useful because I will probably refer to it throughout the next several sessions, looking for items for each to work on during the following week. It will, to a large extent, become the store from which I get materials for discussion and change. It also separates those who are sincere about changing their own lives from those who are not really interested in pleasing God. Those who only seek relief rarely will go along with it. It is an important assignment that I give to most counselees.

Another first session assignment that I often give is to send a couple home to begin learning to communicate with one another as they should. I ask them to set up a conference table at a specific time and place during the week to which they will bring various problems that they need to discuss. I set up rules: no one is to do anything else at the table but to confer. If anyone argues or gets nasty (in words or attitude), the other is to rise quietly (no verbal response is allowed), thereby indicating that "in my opinion we have stopped conferring." The other is to calm him or herself down and then say (politely), "Please sit down so we can continue conferring." No argument is to be given whether they had actually ceased conferring or not.

The conference table is to be called and led by the husband,[2] who reads Ephesians 4:29–32 and then calls on his wife to pray prior to conferring. The conference is to last no longer

---

1 Plainly, I will get concrete items in asking for 100 or more on the list. People don't change in the abstract, but only in the concrete. That is because they live in the concrete, not in the abstract. No one, for instance, is actually "considerate" or "inconsiderate," but does things to which we attach the abstract labels "considerate" or "inconsiderate." Homework assignments ought always focus on concrete changes, not on the labels by which they are known.

2 Thereby placing him in his headship position by taking charge of the spiritual life of his home as its head should.

than half an hour. The results are to be recorded by the wife, who is the secretary, and brought to the next counseling session. When a matter cannot be solved by the couple's consulting the Bible, they are to write out what it was that obstructed this eventuality and bring that to counseling as well.

Sometimes, if they have a hard time understanding how to do these things, I will roleplay what I have in mind, taking the place of either the husband or wife. This is a way of demonstrating that is usually very effective. Roleplaying, however, must be used for the right purpose – instruction.[1]

Homework ought to be achievable. Understanding that in the first session a counselee is new to everything you do, and that he is still struggling with difficult problems, try to choose those assignments that may be easily done if a person really wants to do them. Early success in small ways can lead to large changes in attitude and behavior. Start small and build on the success (cf. Matthew 25:23).

Homework is a tool that helps counselees "flesh out" commitments made in counseling. That is to say, for instance, when one goes and seeks forgiveness of another during the week as the result of an assignment to which he has committed himself (because he wants to please God), counseling takes on a concreteness that mere discussion fails to achieve. He actually sees the results of counseling in his home, at work, or wherever the homework is done. And having to return, whether he succeeds or fails at doing his homework, is important too. If he succeeds, then the success can be reinforced by the counselor and by the next assignment. If he fails, he and the counselor may "take apart" what was done to see what got in the way. In that way, he may even learn through failure, which can be turned into success.

Homework may uncover other underlying problems. It may show laziness, disorganization, procrastination, discouragement, bad attitudes, and the like, which got in the way of fulfill-

---

1 Some use it wrongly for more subtle reasons, usually to cause changes of feeling or attitude in subliminal ways.

ing the assignment. These may be very important, and might not have been brought to the fore had one not failed to do a homework assignment.

Homework is tangible and, therefore, is a way of encouraging one's marriage partner or others. When a spouse "sees" his or her spouse making a genuine effort to do the right thing, it brings hope to him or her. Talk is transformed into action. Usually, when one is making an effort, he will receive encouragement from others; this also helps in the process of change. Moreover, when one begins tangible change, he puts himself "out on a limb." Not only do others see and encourage, they also will hold him to the changes that he has begun to make.

Instead of waiting for a week until the next counseling session for something to happen, homework makes counseling a daily factor – and that is how old patterns are broken and new ones are established (in consistent, daily, repetitive action). Counseling goes on every day in the milieu in which the change is required. That makes counseling concrete as well.

In every way, then, homework is a vital part of counseling. As Jesus said, at the conclusion of the Sermon on the Mount, the one who *hears* His words and *doesn't do them* is like the man who built on sand, while he who hears *and does them* is like the one who built on rock. Homework is one way of helping counselees to get beyond hearing into doing. It is, therefore, of the *utmost* importance to good, biblical counseling.

Chapter Ten

Getting Commitment

Your aim is to get commitment at the outset. That is not always possible – or, at times, even desirable. A person should not commit himself to what you propose in counseling unless and until he understands that it is biblical. To call counselees to commit to anything less is totally wrong for a Christian counselor since the commitment is to God, not to you. There is one exception to insisting on full commitment in the first session: if the person commits to investigating for a week or two whether or not what you are doing is biblical. He may want to ride along for that time to be sure. But even then, there will be elements of what you do (initial homework) to which he must commit himself if he really wants to know whether these things you are saying are all so. His commitment must not be merely intellectual.

Commitment is essential for proper counseling. You must seek commitment to learn and to do God's will. That is fundamental to most other things. Apart from it, counseling will fail. The counselee must be brought to the point of actually saying to you (and remind him that he is saying it before God) that as God gives him the grace, he will do what he should.

What you are interested in avoiding is a half-hearted agreement to "play along" with counseling. Either the counselee will throw himself into the counseling process with all his heart and soul or he should not be allowed to begin. Instead of the problem he came presenting, your new, immediate counseling problem now becomes to convince him that God wants wholehearted commitment.

Commitment is a matter of trust in the promises of God. To call for trust in what you have to say is insufficient. Make it clear, by the way that you open and expound the Scriptures, that you are interested in his doing what God says, and in nothing less.

Full commitment usually involves five things:

1. *Knowledge of what one is getting into.* Here, that means knowing that to the best of his ability the counselor will help the counselee to learn and to do what God, in Scripture, desires of him.
2. *Desire to do it.* While he does not have to like what God requires of him (it may be unpleasant), he must desire to do it in order to please God.
3. *Willingness to get know-how and obtain resources to pull it off.* One may want to make certain changes that he knows he should, but unless he has what it takes to change, it will not happen.
4. *Planning and scheduling.* Unless he actually lays out the plan with dates, he is not likely to get beyond the talking and thinking stage.
5. *Doing it.* All the great plans and fine schedules on paper are not the same as actually getting out there and doing what God requires.

Because each of these elements is essential to a genuine commitment, you must make each clear to the counselee. In addition, you must check him on each element to be sure his commitment is valid. If, for instance, the counselee wants to please God by seeking forgiveness of another whom he has wronged, but he doesn't know what to say and how to say it, he is likely to botch things up. You may have to role play the event with him to see if he has what it takes to ask forgiveness. If he is likely to excuse himself, rather than admit his sin, this will have to be dealt with. If he is likely to accuse the other person rather than confess his sin, that will have to be dealt with. And so it goes.

The sort of commitment that is valid is the commitment that will lead to all of the goals of counseling in the ways that God's Word prescribes. It will mean that the counselee, from his heart in order to please God, will do as the Word requires because he has the know-how and the resources to do it (or is willing to acquire them[1]). It also means the counselee will write a sched-

---

1 Suppose restitution is required, but the counselee does not have the finances

ule and follow it.

What do you do if a person is unwilling to make a wholehearted commitment? Well, short of closing down counseling, you may do a couple of things. First, don't argue about it. Instead, insist on it; say that you can do nothing more until he makes the commitment. In dealing with counselees, you will not budge on this matter of commitment. Moreover, don't assume that a commitment has been made unless you have carefully gone over the five points with the counselee and secured his agreement to all. If he won't commit himself, but has reservations, you may want to postpone future sessions until he has thought things through and wants to resume counseling with proper commitments. You must be careful that he is not resuming counseling because of the pain and hurt alone (often the struggle about resuming counseling will intensify these).

Remind the counselee of Jesus' words,

> If anybody wants to do His will, he will know about the teaching – whether it comes from God or whether what I say comes from Myself (John 7:17).

If your teaching is in line with God's, you can expect God to honor a counselee's sincere desire to know the truth about your method of counseling. In other words, there is no excuse for giving a halfhearted response to counseling and no more than a halfhearted response to Him.

Commitment is basic to counseling, but there is something even more basic. Unless repentance, where it is necessary, comes first, there is likely to be no commitment. Repentance leads to the willingness to commit to hard things. It leads to a desire to please God. It leads to wholeheartedness. Where there is no commitment, you cannot complain when a counselee comes to counseling only when he cares to. You cannot hold him to doing what he ought to do in his homework assignments.

---

to pay back what he owes. Commitment may, in such a case, involve taking a part time job in addition to one's regular job to become financially able to do so.

After all, he never committed himself to do either. We live in a day in which people want to follow their whims rather than their responsibilities. It is an era of non-commitment. It is an era in which people are motivated by the things that they "feel" like doing rather than what they *should* do. So to ask for commitment may be to ask for something unknown to many of your counselees. Explaining the five elements in wholehearted commitment, therefore, is essential.

Since people in this age commit themselves to live together "until death" and then get divorces within the year, it should be obvious that commitment doesn't mean much to them when even such an important commitment is held lightly. You must emphasize that you expect to commit yourself and your time to helping,[1] and that you will expect the counselee to do the same. You may even want to mention the divorce example as the sort of "commitment" that you are *not* talking about. And you might note that if the person has difficulty keeping commitments because of sinful living patterns, you will have to deal with that problem along the way as well as any others. In other words, you will make a "big deal" out of commitment – because in God's eyes that's what it really is!

So because commitment is vital to counseling, you must not make light of it when a counselee fails to keep his commitments. Instead, you must remind him of what he has done and what he needs to do about it. You may also state that you cannot counsel properly unless he begins to keep commitments. You will, in all cases, insist that unfulfilled homework assignments be kept – even when they are a week or more late. In other words, you will not allow counselees to get away with not keeping commitments. You will explain that you cannot move forward until prior commitments are fulfilled.

Of course, we are going beyond the first session in this discussion, but it is crucial to point out many of these things as early as possible so that the counselee begins counseling in the

---

1 That means that you must set a good example of what commitment means: don't cancel sessions, be there on time, and so forth.

right way. To allow him to think that commitment means no more to God than it does to the modern man or woman who forgets all about it when things become difficult is to give a wrong impression that will come back to haunt you later in counseling. Establish things rightly in the first session and you will rarely have problems with those things later on.

Chapter Eleven

A Note on
Closing the Session

Never, *never,* **never** allow the first session to run beyond its allotted time.[1] If you do, you can be sure that this error will set a precedent that you will regret. In session after session, thereafter, your counselee will expect you to do the same. This warning also includes a warning about post counseling chit-chat. At the end of the session, after praying, stand immediately, head for the door, open the door and shake the hand of the counselee as you escort him out. Chit-chat at the door can do two harmful things: it can waste valuable time, and more importantly, it can destroy the mood with which you want to see the counselee depart. Let's talk about that for a minute.

Having reached a climax (high point)[2] near the end of the session, as you move toward sending the counselee out to do his week's homework, you will want to close in prayer. This prayer should highlight the major emphases that you want the counselee to carry away in his mind.[3] Pray about any commitments made, about the week's problems and temptations that he is likely to encounter, about his homework. The "amen" closing the prayer should alert him to stand and head for the door. Make it so from the first session. Remember, you are establishing patterns (that is one key to all that you do in this first session). Chit-chat, as I have called pleasantries and the sort, is anticlimactic.[4] That is, therefore, exactly what you wish to avoid.

---

1 Of course, there are *rare* (I emphasize the word) exceptions. But they should be few and far between. They should be true emergencies; nothing less.
2 From the Greek for "ladder." Throughout the session think of climbing a ladder until at the end you reach the top.
3 Chit-chat tends to dull the sharpness of the emphasis.
4 It is like going down the ladder several rungs!

The climax, or high point, of the session immediately before the prayer ought always to include a note of encouragement. And this should also be given in the form of an exhortation. "Now that you've made that commitment to the Lord, you can expect things to happen as you follow through. Don't let anything stand in your way. Remember, the Lord is concerned about the change that you will be making at work. He will be with you in time of temptation. Just don't allow anything to change your mind. You know that by God's grace you can do it. Now, before you leave,[1] let's pray about all of this...."

When the counselee leaves, be sure that he has taken everything with him. There are counselees who will leave their written homework assignment behind.[2] That is because they are nervous or careless. Others will deliberately do so in order to avoid doing the assignment this week. Whether this is intentional or unintentional is not the point;[3] make sure you look to see that they have the assignment with them as they leave.

---

1 Note the announcement that counseling is over.

2 All assignments ought to be written – by you – so that there will be less misunderstanding later on. The written assignment also acts like a counselor during the week, encouraging the counselee to get busy doing his assignment.

3 In the first session. If it happens again, it might be worth investigating. Some will "lose" their assignments in the car, at home, etc. Check out the reason.

Conclusion

If, after having read this book, you feel like exclaiming with the apostle Paul, "Who is sufficient (*Greek: hikanos*) for these things?" (II Corinthians 2:16), take heart. In the next chapter, Paul writes, "He has made us sufficient (*hikanos*) servants of a new covenant" (II Corinthians 3:6).

I know that it seems hard to imagine doing all that I have described in that first session. But, believe me, it can be done. It takes many words to tell, and many minutes to read about that which can be *done* in a very short time. Moreover, many things can be done in tandem.

For instance, when you are giving a homework assignment and you slip in a reminder that this assignment must be done as the counselee has agreed or you will not be able to go on to other things, you have combined three elements that I have discussed as discrete items. As you are discussing the answer to the agenda question, "What do you want us to do about it," you may also clearly state that God's will must be first on the agenda. While asking questions during data gathering, you will often have opportunities to explain passages of Scripture that relate to the answers you receive. And so on. In other words, reading about and doing various things in the session are two very different things.

Then, too, there is the matter of learning and experience. These speed things up. After a while you will do most of the things in this book without thinking, if you have practiced them. You will respond to each development out of habit. You will have to make fewer and fewer conscious decisions over a period of time. For example, your use of the PDI will become almost automatic. You will know where to look and what to look for in various cases without thinking twice about it.

So don't despair if these things don't happen right away. Keep working with them, and in time you will see everything falling into place.

Now, let's review some things. The first session is important because you set expectations and establish policies and practices in it. It is important because the counselee is making crucial decisions during it: "Will I continue counseling?" "Will I do the homework I have just been given?" "Do I believe that this counseling will really be biblical?" "Is this counselor competent?" Questions like those flow through a counselee's mind. How you conduct the first session may have much to do with the answers that he gives himself. That is one very good reason to work at learning to conduct the first session well.

Much that I have said is suggestion. I expect you to take it and run with it. And read between the lines. Develop those suggestions in your own way. Moreover, in the matter of emphasis and the amount of time you devote to one item or another, you will learn how to adjust to each case. You will spend much time with one counselee discussing the data on the PDI; with another, you will hardly talk about it at all. Some counselees will readily assent to all your conditions; others will balk, drag their feet, or hem and haw. What you will do in each case will vary a great deal, so the time you spend in doing things will vary greatly. Be flexible.

I sincerely hope that what I have written will prove helpful to you. It took me many years to develop and refine the concepts that I have presented here. If the title, *Getting Started*, describes your situation as a person new to counseling, it should put you light years ahead of where I was when I began counseling. I suggest that you review the book each time you are about to begin a new case. If you have been counseling for some time, I may have refreshed your memory about some things that may have slipped by you. I may have challenged some of your present practices or suggested things to add to them. Whatever the case may be, give these ideas some thought. In one way or another, I suspect that you could learn something. I encourage you to try those things you are not so sure about. After trying them in several cases, consider whether or not they make a difference.

CRITICAL STAGES
of BIBLICAL
COUNSELING

Breaking Through
The Turning Point *of*
Biblical Counseling

Jay E. Adams

Breaking Through
The Turning Point
of Biblical Counseling

Contents

Introduction

The first book in this trilogy, *Getting Started: The First Session of Biblical Counseling*, surveys the things that are essential to know and do – as far as possible – in the initial counseling session. The counselor establishes policies, begins practices, and gathers data. This second book is dedicated to that very important period when counseling takes on new life, when it takes a new direction or a new impetus. The key word, as you can see, is the word *new*. There is a change. There is a newness in the counseling that comes from "turning a corner," or from experiencing a "breakthrough," or "getting over the hump," as we say. Up until that time counseling may have been successful in the sense that all the right things were being done – indeed, the very things that may have led to the breakthrough – but radical change had not yet taken place. The turning point in counseling sessions, then, is that point at which the counselor sees the beginning of appreciable, observable change in the difficulty (or difficulties) that were presented and/or uncovered during previous counseling sessions.

When does this change occur? There is no point in time that is common to every counseling case. It could happen at any juncture from the first session (a very rare occurrence) until the seventh or eighth one.[1] There are first sessions when the counselor makes all the difference by providing the very direction the counselee needed but could not find on his own because of his lack of knowledge. A few sessions may follow in order to consolidate the gains made in that initial session, but for all practical purposes counseling has turned the corner during that first session and is headed for completion.[2] Mostly, however, the turning point in counseling will come after several weeks of

---

1 See my discussion of multiple sessions in *Getting Started*.
2 This is another way to describe the turning point in counseling: it is that time from which counseling begins to wind down, often relaxes somewhat, and heads directly for termination.

successive counseling sessions, between which homework[1] is done that often leads toward the turning point.

To be successful in counseling there has to be some point of breakthrough in the case. This is why biblical counselors think about, look for, and plan to bring about conditions that may foster such an event. There may be minor turning points – and, in some cases, that is all that there will be.[2] Ordinarily, though, there is a more-or-less grand transformation that is quite obvious by the difference that it makes, even if it does not take on the nature of a radical change. This change, among other things as we shall see, can be a change of knowledge, of understanding, of determination, of conviction or of commitment. It may follow repentance, successful completion of some homework assignment, a breakthrough in interpretation and application of Scriptural truth, or similar "eureka"[3] moment in counseling.

The turning point may or may not be (though it usually is) known to both the counselor or counselee when it occurs, but it is possible that one or the other (usually the counselee) may not recognize it right away. When that happens, it is often because there have been previous false breakthroughs and the real one is suspected to be simply another of the same kind. When either counselee or counselor protests to the other that "this time it is for real," the other ought to pay particular heed and treat it as though it were the truth. More often than not, when this happens, he will find that it is a genuine breakthrough.

The turning point is crucial to counseling because, as we saw in the previous book of this trilogy, God tells us that His thoughts and His ways are not ours (Isaiah 55:8–9); therefore, we must change in order to begin to think His thoughts after Him and to walk in His steps (as we see them exemplified in

---

1 See *Getting Started,* page 65, for information on homework (also *The Christian Counselor's Manual* where the matter is discussed in depth).

2 A series of minimal but solid changes leading to the solution of the problem(s) may, indeed, be the ideal way to see change come about because it most nearly approximates Christian growth and sanctification, which is gradual and, at times, almost imperceptible.

3 Greek for "I found it!"

Jesus Christ, God manifest in the flesh). This changing of thoughts and ways, we saw also, is the essence of repentance.[1] And the interesting thing is that when God speaks of the need for man's ways to conform to His own, He immediately turns to the Bible as the Source from which to obtain that which is necessary to make the change (Isaiah 55:10–11). In speaking of this Word by which change is effected, God also says that it is *always effective*. He declared that the Word that goes forth from His mouth shall not come back to Him without accomplishing that for which He gave it. It is like the rain and snow that waters the earth and brings forth growth in the plant world. The biblical counselor knows that as he ministers the Word in faith, God will bring about His will (not always the same as ours!) through it. He is not ministering some inert, dead message of man, but the living, powerfully working Word of the almighty God (Hebrews 4:12)![2]

The turning point may take the nature of a major crisis,[3] or it may come more gradually as I mentioned. But whenever it comes, and in whatever form, in biblical counseling it is always precipitated by the application of the Scriptures to the counselee. And the results will be major.

This comes about in various ways. There may be new material presented, new understanding of older information, new

---

1 Repentance has two dimensions. The New Testament emphasizes the change of thought by the use of *metanoia* ("a change of mind; rethinking"), while the Old Testament stresses the outcome of this change of mind by use of the word *shuv* ("a change of direction; turning"). In one sense, the turning point is always a point of repentance since it involves both of these elements.

2 See my book *How to Help People Change* which is a practical application of II Timothy 3:16ff. In this book, I show how the Scriptures were intended by God to change people and how a counselor may use them to do so.

3 The Greek word *krisis*, means "separation., judgment." In "an extended sense," however, says Crabb, it has come to mean "whatever decides or turns the scale" (we would probably say 'tips the scale'). It "immediately precedes a change." George Crabb, *English Synonyms*: New York. Harper and Brothers (1891), p. 247. It is this derived, "extended" sense that controls our use of the term in this book. The idea of a crisis immediately preceding a change is central.

ability to see the application of it to life, or the breaking down of barriers erected against the truth. True Christian change – of the sort that alone pleases God – always involves a closer approximation of the thought and the life of the counselee to the "thoughts" and to the "ways" of God as these are set forth in the Bible. That understanding undergirds all biblical counseling.[1]

---

1 "Breakthroughs" of any other sort – not based on the application of the Scriptures to the counselee – are not only false but will always be harmful since they will involve "insight" about and/or "commitment" to something or someone other than God. Indeed, such change will only lead the counselee into more difficulties. These may combine with the original problem to enlarge or intensify it.

Chapter One

Why Must There be a Turning Point?

The short answer to that question is that, in one way or another, counselees are headed in the wrong direction. This may be the result of ignorance, disobedience, or both. All biblical change involves putting off as well as putting on.[1] Old thinking and old living that was out of accord with God's must be replaced by adopting His new thinking and His new ways (see Ephesians 4:22–32). That is the essence of spiritual growth.[2] But this put off/put on dynamic is not automatic. The new thinking (learned and accepted in the heart) leads to the new living. Because the new thinking doesn't originate in the mind of sinful man, a revelation had to be given to the believer from the absolutely holy and true God so that he could learn these new ways. God gave us that revelation of His thinking and His ways in Jesus Christ, Who "interpreted" God to us[3] as He revealed the mind of God by speaking it and living it. He was the Word[4] made flesh (John 1:14).

Today, we read of Him in God's revelation of truth and righteousness in the Bible. So the mind of God, exhibited in the living Word, Jesus Christ, is clearly portrayed in the words and actions of Jesus, and in the commentaries upon them by the inspired New Testament writers. Man's original, true knowledge, righteousness, and holiness were forfeited in the fall and must be "renewed" (Colossians 3:10; Ephesians 4:24). In counseling, the turning point – with reference to the problem(s) with

---

1 See the *Christian Counselor's Manual* for details.
2 Counseling is interested in helping Christians grow. As we shall see, it is part of the growth process of planting and building.
3 John 1:18; the word translated "revealed" means "exegeted" or "explained."
4 The One in Whom the expression of God's thought became visible and audible.

which the counselor and the counselee have been struggling – is the point at which some element or elements of this renewed knowledge or righteous, holy living break through into the life of the counselee.

What does that mean? Well, it means that at some point there is an understanding or acceptance of what God says in His Word that turns his wrong thinking and living to God's right thinking and living. The breakthrough, then, is a breakthrough by the Spirit of God into the life of the counselee. He Who "moved" the writers of the Scriptures takes those same Scriptures and so burns them into the hearts and the minds of the counselee that they do in him whatever it was that God intended to do by sending His Word (Isaiah 55:11). A turning point in his sanctification has occurred.

Obviously, that cannot happen in an unbeliever because he does not have the Spirit of God dwelling in him. This deficiency means that he can neither understand nor welcome the teachings of God's Spirit by Whom this change is effected through His Word:

> [6]Of course we do speak wisdom among those who are mature, but it isn't modern wisdom or a wisdom that comes from modern day leaders, who are coming to nothing. [7]Rather, we speak about God's secret wisdom that has been hidden, that God predestined before time began for our glory. [8]No modern-day leaders have known this; if they had known they wouldn't have crucified the Lord of glory. [9]But as it is written: "What the eye hasn't seen and the ear hasn't heard, and what hasn't been conceived by the human heart, is what God has prepared for those who love Him." [10]To us God revealed it by His Spirit. The Spirit searches into everything, even the deep thoughts of God. [11]Who knows the thoughts of a person except the spirit of the person in him. So too no one knows God's thoughts except God's Spirit. [12]Now we haven't received the world's spirit but the Spirit Who is from God, so that we may know that which God has freely given to us. [13]It is these things about which we speak, not in words taught by human

wisdom but in those that are taught by the Spirit, combining spiritual teaching with spiritual words.

[14] But a natural person doesn't welcome the teachings of God's Spirit; they are foolishness to him, and he isn't able to know about them because they must be investigated spiritually. [15] But the spiritual person is able to investigate everything while (on the other hand) nobody has the ability to investigate him. [16] "Who has known the Lord's mind? who will instruct Him?" But we have the mind of Christ (I Corinthians 2:6–16, CCNT).

That does not mean that after the breakthrough the believer is entirely changed so that there is no longer any possibility that he may revert to old ways of thinking or living. But it does mean that at this point in his life he has taken a step forward in such a way that he will now be able to overcome and replace some of those old ways with new ones. The change that occurred at this turning point has now enabled him to do so.

Of course, he may have understood and may even have lived according to the new thoughts and ways in time past, but then he *did* revert. In that case, the counsel that he receives must focus not so much on new thinking and new living, but on those biblical truths that will enable him to repent of disobedience and become instead "rooted and grounded" in those truths (Ephesians 3:17). This rooting and grounding takes place when the Holy Spirit "strengthens" him "with power in the inner person" (Ephesians 3:16) so that Christ dwells in his heart by faith (v. 17). In the parallel passage in Colossians, this dwelling is expressed as Christ's *Word* dwelling in him richly as teaching and counseling takes place among believers[1] (Colossians 3:16). Christ works within, through the Holy Spirit Who strengthens him by the Word in those aspects of his life that previously were weak and had not been firmly rooted and grounded. The rooting

---

1 The verse reads, "Let Christ's Word dwell in you richly, as you teach and counsel yourselves as wisely as possible..." (CCNT). The verb here translated "counsel," is *noutheteo*, the New Testament word from which the title "nouthetic counseling" comes.

and grounding imagery has to do with firm planting or building that withstands wind or rain that beats against the plant or structure. It might be thought of as counseling that firms up one's faith.[1] Indeed, it is important to understand this, because much counseling is involved in such rooting and grounding function. So the goal of counseling, in each case, is either to lead to a turning point at which one comes to know some new biblical thinking or living, or to root and ground a counselee so as not to be moved by temptation and sin as he has in the past. The former sort of counseling is largely instructional (the *teaching* of Colossians 3:16) while the latter is largely correctional (the *counseling* mentioned in the same verse).[2]

So the need for a turning point should be obvious. If your counselee has been short on truth (perhaps he has been converted but thereafter has neither been taught well nor sought out truth in personal Bible study[3]) he will largely need teaching. If he has been taught error, the same will be true. So in counseling, the goal is to so present the truth that there will come a time when what the counselor has been saying from the Bible will break into the counselee's consciousness and will effect a turning point. Your prayer should be that the Spirit may use His Word to effect this outcome. On the other hand, the goal of the counselor who is dealing with a disobedient or weak Christian is to bring about repentance and strengthening by the Spirit-empowered Word that will lead to a life of firm obedience. This too begins with the turning point when resistance ceases and strong desire to comply occurs.

---

1 As Paul put it, the rooting and grounding is in "love." Love for God and neighbor comprehends the whole of what God requires of the believer. One will not be moved from this foundation of love if the Spirit "strengthens" him through the Word.

2 This is strictly a matter of emphasis. There are always both in each counseling case if what is done is biblical. *Exhortation* regarding the new teaching and *biblical instruction* about how not to revert are both needed.

3 As may be the case with many who "walk the aisle" but stop walking thereafter!

This turning point – of whichever sort it may be – makes all the difference in the nature of counseling. Before, there may have been foot dragging. Excuses and objections may have been the order of the day for several sessions. Homework may have been done only half-heartedly. The counselee's efforts may have failed due to succumbing to temptation – you name it. But now that there has been a breakthrough, counseling is over the hump. Counseling may run smoothly from now on. While there may still be much to be done in refining understanding and firming up foundations, counseling becomes a pleasure for both counselor and counselee alike.[1] They cooperate, rather than working at cross purposes. They make genuine, lasting gains and solidify them. Principles turn into life. Truth is shored up. Holiness is on the way toward becoming habitual by repeated successes in living for the Lord. Godliness is now becoming easier because discipline has become the pattern. And while there may be much more counseling yet to be done, as well as the possibility of taking on new problems, there is always a marked difference following the turning point.

Even when new problems are encountered and thereafter may have to be pursued to their own turning points, dealing with these will be different from the first. There will be a new sure-footedness on everyone's part that simply did not exist before. The counselee knows that counseling has succeeded in the past; he is now reasonably assured that it will succeed in the future. He now is on better terms with his Lord; he will more willingly enter into the new project than he did the former one because of his new desire to please Him. In other words, the turning point will bring a momentum into counseling that was not there before. So by all means, it is valuable to work toward the turning point, to recognize it when it takes place, and to take advantage of it so you can firm up past gains and move swiftly toward new successes.

---

1 Earlier, it had been largely a struggle for each; one struggling for, the other struggling against change.

Chapter Two

What Leads to It?

I want to discuss five elements that singly, or in various combinations, lead to the turning point. They may not be the only immediate causes, but they stand out plainly as the principal elements. They are:

1. Repentance
2. Learning and understanding
3. Successful, weekly homework
4. A crisis (or series of crises)
5. Commitment (which involves several of the above; see page 70 of *Getting Started*).

Consider **repentance**.[1] To some extent repentance – or some aspect of it – is always involved in bringing about the turning point. Remembering that repentance includes new thinking (through a change of mind) and new living (through a change of direction), it is easy to see that in one way or another it figures into the newness that is involved in a counseling turning point or breakthrough.

How is that? A turning point is always evidenced by newness. An obvious newness in the thinking, in the attitude, in the commitment, or in certain actions enables you to ascertain that a turn has been made. The turning point may be claimed by the counselee or suspected by the counselor during a particular counseling session, but it can only be substantiated by subsequent evidence of the sort just mentioned. So it is important to understand that the turning point and the realization of it by the counselor or counselee may not always occur at the same time. Even a counselee may not recognize that he has turned the corner on a problem as a counselor claims he has until he sees for himself that this is true.[2] But repentance itself is like that. John

---

1 See also page 53 and page 72.
2 Counselor: "I think that you've got it!" Counselee (skeptically) "Perhaps,

the Baptist spoke of "fruit that is in keeping with repentance" (Matthew 3:8). By "fruit" he meant discernible change of some sort that follows the claim. And Jesus once said that you will know whether a person is genuine or not by his fruit.[1] In time, the fruit, or ascertainable evidence of repentance, will always appear when there is true change. When both counselor and counselee understand that a turning point has been reached, they can proceed to counsel in a more relaxed manner. The relaxation will not pertain to work but to the release of tension that takes place.

Sometimes the turning point principally involves a **breakthrough of knowledge**. A counselee may not understand the biblical doctrine of the perseverance of the saints.[2] You have been struggling with him for several sessions about his fear of losing salvation that stems from faulty doctrinal teaching.[3] He cannot seem to comprehend the teachings of several scriptural verses that you have expounded to him. Finally, in summary of the most recent discussion of I Peter 1:3–5, you ask, "Don't you see? It's because your salvation depends wholly on what Jesus did on the cross, and in no sense on what you do, that you cannot lose salvation. You may fail, but *He* cannot. And He guards you by God's power *through faith*, not apart from it. That is to say, He helps keep you believing because faith comes from Him – first, last and always."

Somehow, the Spirit of God takes that summary of what His Word teaches and zings it into your counselee's heart. Almost leaping from his chair, he says, "That's right! Of course! Even my faith comes from Him. So He's the One Who keeps me in

but I'm still a bit doubtful." This happens particularly when a counselee frequently has had hopes before that failed. Of course, the as yet unsubstantiated claim more frequently is made by the counselee.

1 False prophets produce bad fruit (Matthew 7:16) and thereby indicate that there has been no true repentance. Rather, what they produce is of the devil. True repentance produces fruit that is of the Spirit of God.

2 By His grace, God enables true believers to persevere in the faith so as never to lose their salvation.

3 There are other reasons as well.

the faith by keeping faith in me. I cannot stop believing then. Great! I get it." The breakthrough is in the area of knowledge and understanding. How this new understanding of the Word will develop in his life, how in time it will remove his fears will be worked out over the next few sessions. But the breakthrough has come as the result of Scriptural truth brought home to the counselee. From this point on there ought to be change in all sorts of other ways, but the turning point is in the new conception of assurance through biblical teaching about the perseverance of the saints.

Sometimes, it is through the **faithful pursuit of weekly homework assignments** that you reach the breakthrough. How does this look in practice? Consider the following scenario: A husband comes to counseling who has been leading a nearly totally selfish life. His wife, consequently, has threatened to divorce him. He is totally shaken. He seeks your help. He tells the story of what has happened and blames no one but himself. He tells you that God has made him aware of his self-centeredness and that he wants to overcome it but isn't sure how to do so. You work with him first on his agenda making sure that his first concern is to change in order to please His Lord, not merely to win back his wife. This having been done, you set out a course consisting of various assignments calculated to please God by making him a better, more thoughtful, more considerate husband, the spiritual head of his home. After five weeks of assiduously following these assignments at home, on the sixth session he comes in elated, saying, "She's noticed the difference. She says that she really had no intention of leaving me; she only wanted to wake me up. But best of all, I know that in many ways I am now able to please the Lord as I wasn't before." Plugging away at these homework assignments that made him more Christ-like in his concern for others has begun to change him into the new person that regeneration made possible. And it happened through concrete assignments about mundane matters that he followed faithfully.

A **crisis, or series of crises**, may lead to a turning point in a counseling session. For several weeks counseling has been going on at a slow, plodding pace. Progress – but hardly enough – has been made, but the problem which the counselee came complaining about yet remains. You are about to give up on her or insist that she do better work or dedicate herself more fully to the work when at the very next session she says excitedly, "I've gotten over my fear of bridges!" "Really? What happened?" you ask. She then tells you how she had received word that her daughter was in a car that caught fire. The telephoning informant failed to tell her how seriously she was hurt – if at all – before hanging up. So without giving any thought to it, she drove at top speed, taking the shortest route over three bridges, to get to her daughter who was, it turns out, unhurt. This crisis – by which all that you had been teaching her about love being greater than fear – came to the fore in an actual experience. She did, without any homework assignment, what you have been trying to get her to do. Thereafter, there is some shoring up and consolidating of gains to do, but for all intents and purposes the breakthrough has taken place – she has turned the corner![1]

When a person comes for counseling, it is important to **gain commitment** to the goals and to the process because the two are biblical. The commitment is made, of course, not to you but to God. As I said in the first book of this trilogy (page 70), commitment involves five things:

1. Knowing what it is that you are getting into;
2. Desiring it (because you want to please God);
3. Having or obtaining the know-how and the resources to pull it off;
4. Scheduling it for a time and place;
5. Doing it!

The turning point may take place in any one of these areas (which, you can see, are sequential). For instance, a person may know what the biblical change is (he would not enter into it blindly). Indeed, he may desire to see the change take place (to please God – even though the task is not enviable). And he may even have the know-how to pull it off. His problem, however, he

---

1 An actual case.

expresses this way: "You see, I never seem to get around to doing it." You give this response careful scrutiny, finding out exactly what it is that keeps him from doing it. Your investigation turns up the fact that he is a disorganized person who allows the momentary to outweigh the long term. A thorough discussion of the need for determined scheduling and follow-through ensues. You may even turn to Hebrews 11:25, where you show that true faith puts God first and chooses Christ in the long term over something or someone else in the short term. Help about scheduling, about saying "no," about keeping one's promises, and so on, then leads to the turning point. The key in this scenario is that the counselee needs to be committed in every one of the five areas. His intentions are good, his heart is in the right place, but he is destroying his own best intentions and double-crossing his heart by his failure to schedule important, biblical necessities and to follow through by keeping those engagements that he schedules.

You can see that in most of these items the turning point (or breakthrough) came during counseling, but in widely differing ways. You may not know beforehand how it will take place, but you must work for it and look for it. This you do by a regular, systematic, weekly approach toward the goal (or goals) and trust the Lord in His time and way to bring the results. That means that you go on doing the biblical things that are right to do, not attempting to *program* a turning point,[1] but merely faithfully proceeding with the counseling.

---

1 More likely than not, attempts to program a turning point will lead to false "breakthroughs." Since true breakthroughs are brought about by the Spirit, you ought to be able to see that you cannot program it, since you can't program the work of the Spirit of God.

Chapter Three
Some Factors Involved

In the last chapter we looked at some of the overall causes that lead to the turning point in counseling. At the end of that discussion, I said that there was no way to program the turning point since the Holy Spirit is the One Who produces the breakthrough.[1] While that certainly is true, it does not mean that there are not certain elements involved in counseling that may contribute to the breakthrough. The Holy Spirit works in a believer's life through means, rarely, if ever, apart from them. It would be of use, therefore, to look at some of those means that He may choose to use.

These means and methods are not extraordinary. Nor are they specially related to the problems of bringing counselees to a turning point in their counseling. They are, rather, the ordinary

---

1 Some have lauded Puritan counseling. Personally, I believe that their dealings with the "cases of conscience" (as they often called them) involved a wrongly conceived attempt to program change. They were the first psychologizers of religion who attempted to analyze the various steps (or stages) of conversion in order to program conversion accordingly. They thought that regeneration followed certain preparatory actions on the part of the unconverted sinner (for examples of this see Joseph Alleine's *An Alarm to the Unconverted*). These works were urged upon the unconverted in hopes that the Holy Spirit would use them to bring about regeneration. People who went through the rigors of becoming "sensible of their sins," "attempting to renounce all sinful ways," and the like, but who were not regenerated as the result, often became worried and needed counseling about their concerns. (You will notice that the bulk of Puritan counseling had to do with problems of conversion.) The Puritans who propagated this teaching actually *created* their own counseling cases. The Scottish Presbyterian churches that rejected a works-salvation and remained true to the gospel all testified against preparationism. The old United Presbyterian church in this country adopted a testimony against it that, in part, said that preparationism "sets" the unconverted "to work without strength, and gives him no assurance when he is sufficiently prepared for the reception of Christ." Horatius Bonar wrote powerful hymns and preached trenchant sermons against preparationism. In no way do we wish to even approximate this type of Puritan programming.

biblical means and methods that every counselor should be following all the time in counseling as the situation calls for them. Let's take a look at some of them.

To begin with, counseling ought always to be **biblical**.[1] That is to say, it should be conducted in an atmosphere in which the counselee knows at all times that he is being counseled according to the Scriptures. Moreover, as a result, the atmosphere ought to be such that the counselee knows that his every word, thought, and decision is monitored by God Himself, Who is the principal Counselor. It is God, and His Word that he accepts or rejects; it is He Who rebukes, encourages, and disciplines by His Word. When that is the atmosphere, it is clear also that it is the Holy Spirit Who is using the biblical means and methods that the counselor employs, and not merely the counselor himself.

One of the means that biblical counselors use all the time is **instruction**. The Bible is a book of instruction. It is a revelation of God's mind and will to man. A faithful counselor will teach his counselees what God's will is in any given matter. He will not rely on his own opinion or on the ideas of other men. He creates, instead, a biblical atmosphere by his utter dependence on the Scriptures.

Here is a counselee who does not know about her role as a wife. In helping her become the sort of wife that God wants her to become, the counselor will turn to such passages as Ephesians 5 and I Peter 3. But he will not only read these passages; like Jesus on the road to Emmaus,[2] he will "open" and expound them so that she first understands what God is saying, and second, she sees that it is God – not merely the counselor – who says it. The turning point, as I noted in the last chapter, may come as a passage of Scripture is explained and applied. Whether it does or not is not the counselor's fundamental con-

---

1 See page 17 for detailed information on this matter.
2 Luke 24:25–27; 32. Note that it was the Word of God, so explained and applied, that made their "hearts burn within." This is an example of a turning point at which the disciples moved from despair to joy and excitement.

cern. At all costs, he is using the Scriptures to teach, since that is his role as a teacher of the Word.[1] It is the role of the Holy Spirit to use the Scriptures in such ways as He sees fit. He ministers the Scriptures; the Spirit of God employs them for His purposes (cf. Isaiah 55:11). So one of the elements that may lead to a turning point in counseling is the true, faithful teaching of the Bible.

But the Bible informs not only the counselee; it also informs the counselor. In it he reads such commands as "convict, reprove, urge with complete patience and full teaching" (II Timothy 4:2) and "speak these things; urge and convict" (Titus 2:15). The Bible is to be used not only to instruct, it is also to be applied to the lives of counselees in such a way as to **urge and convict** them.[2] A faithful counselor will take these commands to heart.[3] He will use the "full teaching" of the Bible to urge and convict counselees. He will find himself at times saying such things as, "Really, by this time, we ought to be seeing more progress. It isn't enough for you to come here week after week hearing God's Word only to go home and do little or nothing about it. Remember what we saw that James said about works growing out of faith and what Jesus said at the conclusion of the Sermon on the Mount about hearing and doing. It is not wise, and very dangerous, to hear and not do...." It will often be during times of rebuke and bringing of conviction from the Bible that the Holy Spirit will use His Word to turn counseling about. You want the turning point to be genuine. Therefore, you will urge upon the counselee only what the Bible insists upon. The conviction[4] that it brings will often be used by the Spirit as

---

1 See my book *Teaching to Observe* for information on the need for teaching in counseling.

2 There is a mistaken emphasis abroad in the church today that teaches Scripture ought not be applied by the minister of the Word. Supposedly, the Spirit will do so. Nothing could be further from the truth or more harmful to its intended "use" (II Timothy 3:16).

3 He too is being counseled – about counseling – from the Scriptures.

4 "Conviction" does not refer principally to feeling. It is a court term that means "to so prosecute the case against someone as to *convict* him of the

the means of breaking through the barriers that he has erected against change.

Doing **the homework** that one has resisted, or done only halfheartedly, may bring about the breakthrough. The counselee has been instructed in God's will from the Bible. He has acquired all the know-how and the resources necessary to accomplish what must be done. But up until now, for some reason or another, he has failed to do what he knows that he should do (and may even desire to do). It may be because of fear (of consequences or of failure); it may be because of antipathy toward someone else involved; it may be because he wants to continue to receive the pity or other attention that his present, "hopeless" situation provides for him, or something else. But finally, this week, he does his homework. Perhaps it means that he goes to another whom he has wronged and confesses his sin and asks forgiveness. Perhaps he begins to lead his family in Bible study and prayer. Perhaps it is a matter of resigning from a lucrative job that involves cheating customers. Perhaps it is.... You name it. He comes in the next week, having done the hard thing, the thing he resisted, and counseling has already taken a turn. From here on there will be rough spots (and perhaps more turning points about other matters), but it will not be the same. There will be a new relaxed relationship between the counselor and the counselee because of the new relationship between *the* Counselor and the counselee! When a person no longer resists God, counseling begins to go much more smoothly.

There are times, however, when nothing that a counselor does brings about a turning point, when instead a counselee digs in his heels and refuses to do as God's Word says. We are not talking about when he simply doesn't understand what God

---

crime of which he is accused." The Bible, under the power of the Spirit, ministered properly, makes a complete case against one's sinful behavior. The Bible (II Timothy 3:16), the counselor (see passages above) and the Spirit (John 16:8–11) are all said to "convict." Presumably, then, it is the minister of the Word, using the Bible in the power of the Spirit, that brings about conviction. Here again, we see the Spirit using means to effect His desired results.

requires of him. We are talking about the counselee understanding and refusing to do it – and perhaps even saying so! After patient dealings with him, if this is the conclusion, there may come a time when you must stop counseling and initiate **the process of church discipline** outlined by the Lord in Matthew 18:15 and following. This should happen, however, only when all else fails.

I shall not attempt to discuss this process here since I have written an entire book on the ins and outs of church discipline.[1] But let us say that the process takes place, the former counselee repents, and the turning point is reached through church discipline. Then, as in the case of the man in Corinth who was disciplined and put out of the church, counseling resumes (II Corinthians 2:6–8). In these verses, Paul gives instruction about how he is to be treated. In those words ("forgive," "comfort [literally assist] him," and "reaffirm your love to him") the counselor is given clear instructions about what must be done next.

After successful church discipline, the counselee should be supple and pliable. His resistance will have disappeared. He is to be *forgiven*. You must see that the church expresses this forgiveness in unmistakable terms. He is to be "assisted" in whatever ways that are necessary.[2] If one has been "handed over to Satan for the destruction of the flesh" (I Cor. 5:5), you can be sure that he will have had a hard time. He may have been buffeted about by the evil one physically, materially, and financially. The counselor should take note of this and attempt to help him deal with such matters in addition to resuming counseling about whatever was not fulfilled in previous counseling sessions.

Moreover, in II Corinthians 2, the church is told to "reaffirm[3] its love" for him. This is done by full acceptance of the

---

1 *The Handbook of Church Discipline.*

2 *Parakalleo,* the word used in verse 7, is a broad term that means to help him in whatever and with whatever he needs.

3 The word "reaffirm" (*kuroo*) is used only here in the New Testament. It is a technical term that means to reinstate someone into his former position. This

repentant member. Like the Father receiving the lost son, they should "rejoice." They should be willing to fraternize with him, not stand at a distance. They should offer help in whatever ways they can to see that he is fully restored to his position in the church.[1]

Finally, sometimes **deadlines** force action. It may have an effect on bringing about the breakthrough if you have begun by saying something like this in the first session – long before meeting resistance. "Ordinarily, there is significant change by the sixth week. Under normal circumstances, there is no need to meet more than twelve sessions." I have had people remind me of what I said along these lines. When approaching the sixth (or twelfth) session they have said, "I guess I'd better get about doing what I should since next week will be the sixth session." It might be wrong to make too much of this *as a means* of bringing about a turning point in counseling, but when mentioned as I have just suggested – at the outset – it often becomes something that the Spirit may use to bring about the change. If it is used too strongly to "force" the change, the change may turn out to be inauthentic. At any rate, I have noticed that the deadlines set (not in concrete: note the word "ordinarily") may have a good effect when used properly.

In this chapter, I have mentioned a few out of many things normally done in counseling that, without that intention, God may use to bring the counseling to a turning point. In other words, whenever you do anything that is biblical, it is possible that the Spirit, using His Word, may bless to bring about a breakthrough. In this way, in a sense, the turning point may

---

counselee who has been put out of the church and returned repentant is to be reestablished with full privileges of membership, and not as a second-class citizen of the kingdom. You may have to fight for this among others who want to go on punishing him (cf. v. 6).

1 As a member; not as an officer. Only when he once again can fulfill the requirements for elders or deacons in I Timothy and Titus would he be eligible for election to the office. But he will be eligible to be *considered*, as would any other eligible member in good standing.

come as a surprise to you. It was not something programmed; rather, it was the result of the providential work of God, working through normal biblical counseling procedures.[1]

1 This is but an added reason for being sure that all that you do in counseling is biblical.

Chapter Four

What's Over the Watershed?

The turning point in counseling forms a watershed like the Great Divide. Before the breakthrough, because you had not yet crossed over it, the water all ran one way; now it runs in the opposite direction. That, in one way or another, is what I have been saying all along. Prior to reaching the turning point, counseling concerned itself with breaking through whatever walls stood in the way of growth and progress in solving the problems that were introduced by the counselee or uncovered by the counselor. Following the turning point, at which the wall was breached, the concern now becomes that very growth and progress that you have contemplated all along.

Take an example. Joan, a new convert, just joined your church. However, she has an attachment to a young man who claims to be a Christian but will not make a profession of faith and unite with the church.[1] He wants her to leave the church that she has just become a part of because "they have not encouraged the relationship between us." Of course, the reason for this is that if she continues it, she may end up disobeying God by marrying someone who does not profess faith in Christ.[2] The command in the next to the last verse of I Corinthians 7, "marry only in the Lord," is your basis for discouraging marriage between believers and unbelievers. In the final analysis, having

---

1 Thereby treating himself as if he were, as Jesus in Matthew 18:17 put it, a Gentile and a tax collector (i.e., outside the church).

2 For him to claim salvation, but to refuse to unite with Christ's church and thus submit to its care and discipline, leaves you no alternative but to discourage the relationship. Of course, in the meanwhile, you will try to win him to Christ. But so long as he remains outside the church, he must be treated *as* unsaved (regardless of his actual condition).

been thoroughly instructed about these matters, what she is struggling with is whether to obey or to disobey God. After several sessions, she finally determines to submit to the Scriptures, regardless of the outcome. From that point on in the counseling things are different; the water begins to run the other way. No longer are you rowing against God's stream, but you and she are both in the same boat, flowing with it. That is what I mean when I have described the post-breakthrough period as one in which everyone "relaxes." This is not a relaxation of effort, but it involves a resting in God's will as it is set forth in the Bible. There is no more questioning of it, no more resisting it. Now, it is a matter of how best to do as He requires. Counseling will be conducted on a new note.

This is important to know about because of the changes that it will make in the counselor and in his approach to his counselee. While all along, the counselor has attempted to be a companion who is cooperating with his counselee, the counselee may have viewed the situation differently. In his eyes, the counselor may have seemed more of an adversary. Now, the newness brings about a new relationship that has been the goal for which the counselor has been striving. He doesn't want to be adversarial; yet, at times (prior to the breakthrough) he has found himself in that position. Now true cooperation can take place.

Because the counselor has had to urge and rebuke and convict on the first side of the great divide, he must now take a new tack since he is on the other side at last. He will be no longer the one who stands against much that the counselee wants to do, and stands for much that he doesn't want to do. Instead, he will now have to position himself alongside the counselee, instructing, answering good questions, helping to lay plans, encouraging, and helping him up when his attempts fail. Severe warnings are no longer necessary; now enthusiastic cheers urging him onward take their place. The type of ministry he must exert has changed. Counselors who fail to see this, and fail to adapt to the change, will find that by continuing as they did before the summit was reached they will discourage the counselee rather than help him. He has made a breakthrough. Time to rejoice! Do it.[1] And from then on, recognize that you stand beside, rather than before or behind,[2] the counselee. So a turning point is a change that calls for change. The change on the counselee's part will be apparent. Your change, or lack of it, will also be apparent.

It is important, however, to understand that even though you have reached a watershed moment, there is much more work to do, and the counselee is not, because of his success, thereby rendered sinless. No, he is still the sinner that he was before, even though in one dimension he may have made a quantum leap. There will still be times when you must oppose his thoughts or actions with biblical alternatives; there will be times he will struggle with other issues. There may even be other walls that must be breached – not so significant as the great divide he has crossed – but nevertheless, of importance and difficulty. Once he has conquered that dominating barrier, you will both take a different approach to other obstacles. He knows that since he has succeeded in the greater task, he can also succeed in the lesser. If he fails to see this, you may point it out to him. The first success, then, should produce hope. He ought to be greatly encouraged by how God's Word has made a real difference in his life in the past so that he will trust that Word with far more certainty in future endeavors.

All of these things are part and parcel of success. One thing leads to another – and so on. As his sin spiraled him downward,

---

1 At the time of a breakthrough, I have found myself actually standing up and shouting for joy! I have at times reached over the desk to shake hands with the counselee in congratulation. It would not be amiss, under the right circumstances, to have a Coke on it or something of the sort. Certainly, you will pray in thanksgiving and gratitude. None of these things have I ever planned to do; to do so might be artificial. Yet I have done them all. I have simply let my joy take its natural course in context. In some way, let the counselee know that you recognize that there has been a turn of events that calls for celebration. When he knows that you recognize the change, he too will be prepared for a new relationship with you.

2 The former to block any unbiblical ways; the latter to nudge him into the right ones.

one failure leading to another, so his mood and his failure record increased. Now that he is moving in the opposite direction, success breeds success, and a new mood to boot. Capitalize on this momentum. Set before him some of the other smaller items that you have had on the agenda column of your Weekly Counseling Record[1] items that are readily achievable, and start piling up success after success. In the light of the changed mood, now is the time to plunge ahead with unrelenting speed. Take advantage of the momentum that the breakthrough has generated. Don't let the fire grow cold. Now that you are going downhill (in the good sense of that phrase), the going should be easier; take advantage of that fact. If counseling lags from this point on, rather than increasing, that is probably your fault. This is no time for you to sit back and take it easy. You have lots of work to do, and you will be wise to do it quickly.

I Thessalonians is a book in which Paul commends the church for its love and its growth. There is hardly any condemnation such as is found in other letters. In fact, he even expresses amazement at how well the message was received and what they had done with it (vv. 1:5–10). They loved deeply, since God had taught them how to do so (4:9). Well, then, what is it that the apostle Paul could exhort the church to do? He wants them to do more of the same (3:12)! Once the ball is rolling, he urges that they keep up the momentum. Throughout this letter, you get this message: "You are doing quite well; so do even more, even better!" That is the attitude that you should adopt as a counselor who has reached the turning point. It is that of the coach who sees his team playing well, but recognizes that even so, they are not playing up to capacity. He cheers, but he also urges them on to greater heights.

I stress this because once the initial enthusiasm dies down the counselee, thinking that he has done the one thing he came to do, may want to slow down or even stop counseling. Obviously, there are ways of taking advantage of the momentum, but

---

1 For more on the WCR, see page 29.

only when it still has power to carry the counselee forward. Don't let it fade.

Moreover, you will both have to work to confirm the gains you've already made. You must establish new patterns to replace the ones the counselee is turning away from. That doesn't happen overnight. Fruit takes time and cultivation to grow. You will discover that it probably will take at least six weeks of daily, disciplined practice to replace old sinful habit patterns with new biblical ones. Don't let the counselee think that all the work has been done. He is just over the crest of the hill; he must still cross territory to reach the biblical destination that lies before him.

So, counselor: breakthroughs, turns in the right direction, watershed moments are wonderful and deserve all the enthusiastic rejoicing that they should get. But remember that you have not finished counseling. There is much to be done. Encourage the counselee to take advantage of the momentum that the breakthrough has engendered and *complete the work!*

Chapter Five

What About Failure?

Does biblical counseling ever fail? Well, from one perspective, certainly yes. From another, "never." What does that mean? It means that while counselors and counselees often fail, God, and His promises in His Word, never do. Moreover, as we have seen in Isaiah 55:11, God declares that when His Word goes forth it never returns having accomplished nothing. Indeed, it always accomplishes that which He intended it to accomplish – even when that is not what we expected or wanted.

In a possible allusion to this passage in Isaiah, the writer of Hebrews spoke about the rain which falls and brings about two quite different results. This rain brings forth either thorns and thistles or good fruit. The rain is the same, but the ground upon which it falls makes the difference (Hebrews 6:7–8). There, of course, he was speaking of the preaching of the gospel which was received in faith by some and rejected in unbelief by others. The example had to do with the fact that there are in the church false professors who really do not believe the message, whose lives ultimately demonstrate their unbelief. It was (and is) a warning to all such persons. They may be around Christians, enjoying all the benefits of the "coming age," but they still will not believe. The preaching of the Word, accomplishes its purpose in such persons as it reveals their unbelief.

This very problem may be one reason why there are failures in Christian counseling. The Word of God may be ministered in clarity and faithfulness. The counselor may not have failed, and you can be sure that God did not. When the Word is ministered in such instances, it may well serve the negative end of revealing the lack of true faith and salvation in a counselee. Probably there are more persons who come for counseling who are not genuine Christians than we realize. They fill in the PDI (see page 22) stating that they are saved, but they deceive both themselves and the counselor in doing so. In God's mercy, it may take failure in counseling to reveal that they need to come to faith in Christ. The fact that they fail to do the homework (either because they refuse to, or in some way are not able to) may be the very thing that brings their unbelief to light. As the counselor probes to find the reason why the homework was not done, and why there has been no turning point in counseling, he may at length uncover this important fact. In doing so, the opportunity to trust Christ may be given as the counseling session turns into an evangelistic encounter. Unbelievers cannot be sanctified (grow in spiritual maturity).[1] Paul explains that "Those who are in the flesh [the unregenerate] *cannot* please God" (Romans 8:8). Since this is true, we may say that the "failure" was a success in bringing to light the need for salvation. If he believes, it is likely that "counseling" was the means that God used to uncover that need and to bring the "counselee" into the faith. If this occurs, this – the greatest breakthrough of all – will lead to genuine counseling thereafter.

Sadly, not all whose unbelief is revealed by failure come to faith. Many go on in their unbelief, turning away from Christ, declaring that the counseling (or a counselor) was a failure. Well, in the sense that it started out on the false premise – namely, that the "counselee" was sanctifiable because he was regenerate – this is true. This false premise was accepted because the person was a member of a Bible-believing church, and because he declared on the PDI that he was a believer.[2]

So, in such cases, may we say that there was failure? Again, yes and no. Yes, in that the counseling failed to reach a turning point that solved the presenting problem; no, in that God's purpose for the ministry of the Word was achieved (unbelief was brought to light). If the person, coming to recognize that he had

---

1 Remember, counseling is one aspect of the ministry of edification, which has as its purpose sanctification (cf. Titus 1:1).

2 Presumably, he also had deceived the congregation that received him (something that prompted the discussion of the presence of unbelievers in congregations in the book of Hebrews).

never been saved, then believes after receiving the presentation of the gospel, his fundamental problem[1] *would* be solved. And the greatest turning point of all – conversion – *would* have occurred. So it is possible that failure, in the end, may be turned into success. Isn't that what God, through Jesus, did on the cross? Didn't the seemingly greatest failure of all end up actually the greatest success? God is in the business of turning tragedies into triumphs. And He does so frequently in counseling sessions. Speak to any biblical counselor who has been at it for any length of time and he will have stories to tell you of conversions in "counseling" sessions.

But, as I said, not all whose unbelief is revealed by failure in counseling come to faith. Indeed, it may be possible that the majority do not. These will often go away from counseling telling others that you are a failure, that biblical counseling doesn't work, and the like. You will not convince such persons that it was they who failed, that they misrepresented the facts in their case, and that, consequently, they could not receive from counseling whatever it was that they wanted. You will have to put up with such misinformation that they may spread about, understanding that an unbeliever simply cannot welcome God's truth (I Corinthians 2:14).

There is, however, a responsibility that falls upon your shoulders. You must see that his congregation (elders) are informed of what has happened, so that they can take appropriate measures to help the member either come to Christ or leave the body because of the unbelief that was revealed.

There are, however, times when the unbelief of the counselee is only suspected, but not established.[2] In such cases, you

---

1 Deeper and more basic that any other he could possibly present.

2 It is established by 1) his open statement of unbelief; 2) deliberate refusal to do as God requires, leading to church discipline that ends in his being put out of the church (I Corinthians 5:13); or 3) his leaving the church (I John 2:19). All of these indications come from one's relationship to the church of Christ; no individual on his own may declare that a member of a Bible-believing church is an unbeliever. He may suspect, may warn, may call for investigation, etc., but only the church has the power of the keys.

may have to put counseling on hold to discuss and/or investigate the matter further. The congregation may have to become involved officially.

There are also times when the counselor is a failure. Unlike faith healers, who always blame the person who is not healed for his lack of faith, the biblical counselor is willing to honestly own up to it when he has failed. There are so many ways in which he may fail, that it would be unprofitable to spend time mentioning them here. I suggest that the reader obtain a copy of the *Fifty Failure Factors* that I have compiled and printed in the backs of both *The Christian Counselor's New Testament* and *The Christian Counselor's Manual*. These are always good to have on hand to review in times of failure. But they may serve a preventive purpose as well. Reading them over once a week would remind a person of matters to be concerned about in counseling.

There is no doubt that a counselor often fails in one way or another. But it is always possible to recoup. The way to do this is to acknowledge to the counselee where you have failed, tell him that you intend now to do as you should have, and begin right away. A straightforward approach like this will bring salutary results in most instances. Never bluff. Counselees may not know many things, but they have an uncanny way of knowing when a counselor is bluffing. Besides, bluffing is dishonest and dishonors God. You are fallible; therefore, from time to time, you will fail. Moreover, by the straightforward way in which you handle failure before the counselee, he learns a lesson. He sees, before his very eyes, an example of humility and honesty, which – should God so use it – may bring about a breakthrough in the case.

There are times when both the counselor and the counselee have failed. This usually comes to light around the sixth week, if not before. At this time (40 days and 40 nights after counseling has begun[1]) if no appreciable change is apparent, I usually bring everything to a screeching halt. I say something like this:

---

1 In Scripture, the number 40 seems to indicate a transition period.

"Well, it has been six weeks since counseling began. The fact is that by now, under ordinary circumstances, we should have approached or reached a turning point in the counseling. Something is wrong. Let's stop and analyze what has been happening to see whether the problem is with me, with you, or with both of us." This procedure usually has a marked effect upon the counselee. He will tell you what he thinks is wrong – and often, he is on target. Because you have included the possibility of your failure in what you say, he is more likely to open up about his own. It also gives you an opportunity to show where you may have been too lax, too soft, too apprehensive about stating what you really think, etc. It gives you an opportunity to note any factor that you may have omitted, and to work on that from then on. In other words, an assessment at this point is good and useful in many ways.

As the investigation of a counselee's failure to do homework may reveal other unknown problems (see *The Christian Counselor's Manual* for more on this), so may a six-week failure analysis. It is also possible that no failure has occurred. The situation may be especially intricate, the counselee particularly slow in understanding and assimilating truth, and so on. Then patient persistence is called for. That, too, is important to discover.

All in all, the idea of failure ought to be considered with care. It is not always the indication of bad counseling, and under most circumstances, even when it is, there are ways of turning your counseling around. In other words, failure can become a turning point for the *counselor*!

Chapter Six
Couples' Breakthrough

It is an infrequent occurrence to find that a husband and wife simultaneously reach the turning point in counseling. More often one or the other makes a breakthrough first. Then there are those cases when only one reaches a turning point. The other never does – at least in the same series of counseling sessions. Here, then, are a significant number of possibilities, most of which are not all that pleasant or easy to handle. It is important, therefore, for you to understand some of the angles from which to approach them.

Take first the situation where, because they were working together, both husband and wife turn the corner at the same time. When this happens, it is most likely to occur when they are working on solving communication problems. That is because it takes two to communicate. If the two are both working hard at learning to communicate God's way (cf. Ephesians 4), it is possible for the breakthrough to occur for both husband and wife simultaneously, because when communication is established (or reestablished) it is established for *both*. That is the happy scenario that will often take place. But because communication is essential to solving other problems, in many cases, the establishment of communication is not so much of a breakthrough *in terms of the presenting problem* but, rather, it is a lesser breakthrough that may or may not evolve into a solution to the larger difficulty.

Nevertheless, a joint communication breakthrough is to be treated as a significant advance not only because it allows for communication concerning larger issues, but simply because it *is* a breakthrough. This encourages the couple and also gives them a structured method for dealing with other matters. The conference table (see page 67 for more information) is often the structure within which the communication breakthrough takes place. It may continue to be used as a method for tackling subsequent problems. In learning to communicate, the husband and wife have also learned something about how to solve problems (that is one of the things that is done at the table). That learning experience also provides structure (as well as success) for dealing with these larger issues.

Other issues may loom large, and people may wish to avoid solving the communication problem first; they want to get right to "the main issue." That is a trap that you must not fall into. Many, if not most of these problems, remaining unsolved for some time, have led to the breakdown in communication. But when communication disappears, all sorts of other complications are likely to crop up. For instance, husband and wife begin to suspect one another. They attribute false motives and goals to one another, and so on. Often, these can get so closely attached to the presenting problem(s) that there is no easy way to disentangle them. The way to begin is by reestablishing communication in which many of these flawed perceptions of each other may be dispelled.

Moreover, in many cases, the communication problem has grown so large that it is every bit as significant a problem as any other. So counselor, for these and other reasons, always work on establishing good communication between a husband and wife before launching out into deeper waters. If you don't, you will probably watch, to your dismay, as they undo in a week or two breakthroughs that they made in other issues.

What do you do if only one spouse reaches a turning point? In such cases, you help the non-compliant spouse to see what an opportunity God has provided by this occurrence. Now is the time for him or her to strike while the iron is hot. Tell the counselee, "If the train is pulling out of the station, now is the time to hop on it. Don't wait until it is too late." Stress the hope that the breakthrough in one's spouse ought to give. Urge him to get involved by helping to remove the log jam. In other words, stress the need to "buy up the opportunity." You may even enlist the help of the compliant one to encourage a breakthrough. If then, after patient work, the reluctant spouse continues to refuse to take advantage of the opportunity afforded him, you may find it necessary to institute church discipline.[1] The counselee who has reached a turning point must always be cautioned to be patient. And he or she must not castigate the other for not proceeding at a rate equal to his or her own. All pride or sense of superiority must be guarded against. It is very easy to begin to look down on another person because he or she has not yet come along. Also, watch out for emerging pride, self-righteousness and over-confidence. Remind the growing counselee of I Corinthians 10:12: "So then, let the one who thinks that he stands watch out lest he fall." Here, comparisons are odious. They not only stink, but they may greatly impede progress or destroy all hope of it. Caution the compliant counselee to be helpful, and to be sure that this help is given in a way that avoids every semblance of superiority (see Galatians 6:1–5).

The goal is to bring the counseling to a turning point for both counselees. Apart from that, counseling will falter. Yet it is your task to see that discouragement doesn't set in for either spouse. When one begins to blame matters on the other, remind him that he is to do what God says – whether the other does or not. Neither one is to obey God in order to get his way with the other person. He is to do it to please God – period.

The compliant person should be given directions on how to be helpful to his or her spouse. If you do not do this, you may find that even good intentions of the one may be misinterpreted by the other. When both know what each is to do (because it has been discussed in counseling), that expedient goes a long way toward eliminating much possible confusion.[2]

On the whole, it is right to say that when one spouse is making progress, that spouse must not be held back by a lack of

---

1 Keep in mind that church discipline always *follows* (never precedes) church care, which includes counseling. And remember that it is a blessing as well as a right to which God has entitled every member of His church for his benefit. To withhold discipline when it is called for is to deprive a delinquent member of a basic right of membership. Its purpose is remedial, not punitive. The negative aspect (dismissal from membership) comes only when all of its positive provisions have been exhausted with no positive responses from the offender.

2 Your *immediate* counseling goal for the non-compliant counselee may have

response in the other. Keep the growing one progressing through assignments calculated to help him or her, just as you would if he or she were the sole counselee. With reference to the other, your task is to continue such biblical counseling as the Spirit might possibly use to bring about a turning point in his or her life.[1]

---

to shift from other issues to solving the problem of procrastination, resistance, discouragement or whatever it is that seems to be the reason(s) for his reticence.

1 In regard to details about dealing with husbands and wives, see my *Solving Marriage Problems* and *Christian Living in the Home* for more help. In relationship to failures of the parties to respond biblically, see my *Marriage, Divorce, and Remarriage in the Bible.*

Chapter Seven

Resisting, Rethinking, and Reverting

At the conclusion of the previous chapter, in a footnote, I alluded to the problem of resistance where I suggested that at some point the focus of your counseling may have to change to a consideration of that problem. Sometimes this is true in counseling couples, but it often happens in counseling others as well. It is, therefore, quite necessary to consider this matter before going on.

Resistance may take place for any number of reasons. It is not proper to conclude that it is always the result of sheer disobedience – unwillingness to do as God has commanded. Sometimes it is due to discouragement, sometimes to misunderstanding, sometimes to uncertainty or fear. It is important, above all other matters, to ferret out the *cause* of the counselee's failure to move ahead. That is because different causes require different solutions. Reserve any judgment about disobedience until you have exhausted all other considerations.[1]

If, for instance, fear predominates,[2] it will do little good merely to exhort to obedience. While exhortation must never be neglected, the fear – and the reasons for it – should be explored. Then these fears should be allayed by ministering those passages of the Bible that pertain to it (such as Genesis 3:10; Prov-

---

1 Or until the counselee himself declares that he is willing to disobey God's Word regardless of what you may do or say. Even then, the counselee may be coupling disobedience with fear or some other reason. Be *sure* that you have disentangled all such complicating problems. The declared disobedience may be the result of fearing consequences, etc.

2 One of the most common problems leading to resistance, and a very powerful and debilitating emotion, is fear. It may take the form of the fear of consequences, fear of people, fear of harm. Every counselor must learn to deal with this formidable problem or he will not be able to help many of his counselees.

erbs 10:24, 29:25; Matthew 10:26–31; II Timothy 1:7; Hebrews 2:14–15; I Peter 3:6, 13–14; I John 4:18). Notice I spoke of "ministering" these passages to the counselee. That means more than simply quoting them. It means explaining these passages and showing how they relate to his particular situation. Always, in using Scripture, it is wise to do this unless the counselee gives clear evidence of knowing already what you would say to him.[1]

Resistance may stem from widely differing causes. I shall not go into these, but simply warn that your counselee may be grappling with discouragement,[2] with misunderstanding or with something else. Sometimes, it is misunderstanding that stands in the way of progress by the resistant counselee. He may have misunderstood the Bible or your explanation of it. He may even think that there is contradiction between what you are requiring and what he understands the Bible to say (as we shall see presently may have been the case with Peter). In such a case, it would be his loyalty to God (as he best understands it) that makes him resist![3] Help to straighten him out about such matters. Some may resist simply because they do not know what to

---

Fear may also lead to obsessions such as fear of germs, etc. See my pamphlet *What Do You Do When Fear Overcomes You?*

However, supposed fear in some cases is manipulative, not genuine. Proverbs 22:13, which pictures the sluggard who makes excuses that he is afraid when he really wants to stay home rather than go to work, is an example of this. Learn to distinguish the two. Often, as in Proverbs, this may be done by examining the factuality of the reason given.

1 Even then, reminding him may be important (cf. II Peter 1:12–15).

2 On this problem see II Corinthians 4 to discover how Paul persisted even in those situations that most would consider utterly discouraging (see II Corinthians 6:4–10; 11:23–28). Verse 1 of chapter 4 shows how his sense of gratitude for the mercy of God toward him drove him on in spite of afflictions: "Therefore, since we have this service to perform as the result of mercy, we don't give up." If a counselee thinks that "there is no use" he may resist doing homework. In such cases, I Corinthians 15:57–58 may prove valuable. Be sure to "minister" the verse.

3 To accuse him of disobedience would be a frightful mistake. He may be very wrong in his interpretation or application of Scripture, but his attitude and faithfulness to God may be untarnished.

do or how to obey the biblical command. They may also need greater understanding of what God wants them to do. In such cases, you should be sure that your explanations have been clear. If they haven't, they must be clarified. If, on the other hand, the counselee finds it hard to understand – as some who are greatly confused do – you may have to rephrase or reword your instructions until they "get it." And, in some instances, there are those who simply do not know how to implement a biblical command. You must help them with suggested implementations, and show them how it is done for future reference. In other words, there are all sorts of reasons (some legitimate, some not) why one may resist obeying what to you is a plain command of the Bible.

One of the most interesting examples of resistance in the Bible is found in the story of Peter in Acts 10:

> [1]Now there was a certain man in Caesarea named Cornelius, who was a centurion and belonged to what was called the Italian Cohort. [2]He was a devout man who feared God, together with all his household, and he gave liberally to people in need and regularly prayed to God. [3]About three o'clock in the afternoon he saw an unmistakable vision of an angel from God coming in and saying to him, "Cornelius." [4]He stared at him in terror and said, "What is it, Lord?" And he replied, "Your prayers and your charity have ascended as a memorial before God. [5]Now, send men to Joppa and bring back Simon, who is called Peter. [6]He is staying with Simon the tanner, whose house is by the sea." [7]When the angel who had spoken to him left, he called two of his servants and a devout soldier who was one of those who assisted him, [8]explained everything to them and sent them off to Joppa.
>
> [9]Now the next day, about noon, as their travels brought them close to the city, Peter went up onto the roof to pray. [10]He grew hungry and wanted something to eat. But while they were preparing a meal, he went into a trance. [11]He saw the sky opened, and a sort of container like a huge sheet was being let down onto the earth by

its four corners. [12]In it were all kinds of animals, and reptiles and birds of the sky. [13]A voice spoke to him, "Get up, Peter; kill and eat them." [14]But Peter said, "Oh no, Lord! I haven't ever eaten anything common and unclean." [15]Then the voice spoke to him a second time, "Don't treat as unclean what God has cleansed." [16]This happened three times, then immediately the container was taken up into the sky.

[17]While Peter was inwardly wondering what to make of this vision, just then the men that Cornelius had sent arrived at the gate and asked for directions to Simon's house. [18]They called out, asking if the Simon, who was called Peter, was staying there. [19]So while Peter was still pondering over the vision, the Spirit said to him, "See here, three men are looking for you. [20]Get up and go down and accompany them without hesitation, because I have sent them."

[21]So Peter went down and said to the men, "All right, I'm the one you are looking for; what is it that you have come for?" [22]They said, "Cornelius, a centurion who is just and fears God, who is well spoken of by the whole Jewish nation, was directed by a holy angel to send for you to come to his house and to listen to what you have to say." [23]So he invited them in to be his guests.

The next day he got up and went off with them, and some of the brothers from Joppa went with him. [24]The next day he arrived at Caesarea. Cornelius had been expecting them and had called together his relatives and close friends. [25]When Peter entered, Cornelius fell down at his feet and worshiped him. [26]But Peter made him get up and said, "Get up. I too am a man." [27]And he talked to him as they entered, where he found many had gathered. [28]Then he said to them, "You know that it is unlawful for a Jewish man to associate with or to visit a foreigner. Yet God has shown me that I shouldn't call any man common or unclean. [29]So when I was called, I came without argument. Let me ask, then, why you called for me."

[30]Then Cornelius said, "Four days ago, about this hour – at three o'clock in the afternoon – I was praying in my house when, then and there, a man in bright clothing stood before me. [31]He said, "Cornelius, your prayer has been heard, and your charity has been remembered by God. [32]Send to Joppa for Simon who is called Peter; he is staying in Simon the tanner's house that is by the sea." [33]So at once I sent word to you, and you were kind enough to come. Now, then, we are all here present before God to hear everything that the Lord commanded you."

[34]Then Peter opened his mouth and said, "I can see now that God isn't a respecter of persons. [35]Instead, in every nation, whoever fears Him and practices righteousness is acceptable to Him. [36]The message is the one that He sent to the sons of Israel, preaching peace through Jesus Christ – He is Lord of everything. [37]You know what happened throughout all Judea, starting at Galilee after the baptism that John preached – [38]how God anointed Jesus of Nazareth with the Holy Spirit and power, how He went about doing good and healing all those who were overpowered by the devil, because God was with Him. [39]We are witnesses of everything that He did in the Jews' country and in Jerusalem. They killed Him by hanging Him on a tree, [40]but God raised Him up on the third day and had Him appear, [41]not to all the people, but to us who were previously chosen by God to be witnesses. We ate and drank with Him after He rose from the dead. [42]He ordered us to preach to the people and to testify that He is the One Whom God designated to be Judge of the living and the dead. [43]To Him all the prophets bear witness that everybody who believes in Him will receive forgiveness of sins through His name."

[44]While Peter was still speaking these words, the Holy Spirit fell on all those who heard his message. [45]The believers from the circumcision who had come with Peter were astounded that the gift of the Holy Spirit had been poured out on the Gentiles too [46](they heard them speaking in various languages and exalting God). Then

Peter said, [47]"Nobody could refuse water to baptize
these people who have received the Holy Spirit just as
we have, could he?" [48]So he ordered them to be baptized in the name of Jesus Christ. Then they asked him
to stay for a few days.

As you can see, Peter's resistance (v. 14) was to the Lord
Himself![1] God told him (through the voice from heaven) to eat.
In his utter confusion, Peter said "No." That is resistance. And,
it seems that the resistance was so strong that the Lord had to
tell him three times to eat before he did (v. 16). The resistance
was strong, I say, because this was a *direct* encounter with *God*,
and Peter knew it (He says, "Oh no, *Lord*"). Yet three times
Peter refused to eat! But God did not give up on Peter. Why?
The reason is that, in his confusion – and there surely must have
been much – he thought that he was being asked to do something that he had refused to do all his life out of *obedience* to
God.[2] So Peter resisted, giving as his reason: "I haven't ever
eaten anything uncommon or unclean." He thought that there
must be some sort of contradiction. But the contradiction, as in
all such cases when the counselee knows what the Lord requires
of him and resists, is that he thinks that he knows God's will
better than others – better than what God *Himself* says in the
Bible. I have had people say, "I know that is what the Bible
seems to say, but it can't be that. There *must* be some other
explanation. God couldn't require that of me." And, though they
may think it is, the biblical requirement isn't in any way as

---

1 Remember, if the atmosphere in counseling is correct, your counselee will
always know that his resistance is against the Lord rather than you. So the
story of Peter is certainly applicable to what you may find in counseling sessions.

2 For the opposite reaction in similar circumstances, see the case of Abraham
(Genesis 22:1–10) who was told to sacrifice Isaac, his only son – the son of
promise – and the case of Hosea (Hosea 1:2–3), who was told to marry a pros-
titute. Both responded immediately, in faith. Hebrews tells us how Abraham
reasoned (see Hebrews 11:17–19). On Peter's response, see also (Matthew
16:22–23), where there is a similar response given out of what he (mistakenly)
thought was proper.

seemingly contradictory as this one given to Peter. It usually has to do with a false interpretation of the Bible.

So Peter's resistance is clear. But the voice from God persists (that is what you must do too).[1] He makes it clear that a new era is at hand. He says, "Don't treat as unclean what God has cleansed" (v. 15). God has now cleansed the Gentiles (Acts 15:9) [just as He lifted the dietary laws; Mark 7:19][2] and the gospel must be taken to them. Moreover, it meant that in order to present the gospel Peter would have to enter the house of a Gentile and eat his non-kosher (non-"clean") food. These were two things forbidden to Jews.

Finally, after wondering about the matter, and after the arrival of the men sent by Cornelius (vv. 17–20), Peter began to put it all together (v. 28). After Cornelius' explanation (vv. 30–33), and the giving of the Spirit (v. 44), Peter understood even more elements of what was happening. He was in the process of **rethinking** (remember the word *metanoia,* "repentance," means: "to rethink, to change the mind"). Peter thought that he understood, but he had not. Now the full meaning of the keys (Matthew 16:19) was going to become a part of his understanding as well. As he had been given the privilege of opening the door to the New Testament church to the Jews, so now he would use the second key to open the door of the church to the Gentiles. By the time Peter had to explain to others what had happened; he had it together at last (Acts 11:1–18).[3]

What you have just looked at is a fine example of an apostle who had to reach a turning point in his life in order to minister properly. The breakthrough took place, but it took a revelation from God to achieve it. Similarly, there is no reason to expect that there will be a turning that will be adequate and that will last unless it comes from the understanding and the acceptance

---

1 By means of careful exposition of the Bible so that the counselee sees clearly that *God* is requiring what you are insisting upon, and not merely you, yourself.

2 A word from Jesus that Peter had not understood before.

3 Note, especially, how the Old Testament figured into his new understanding (Acts 10:42, 43).

of God's revealed truth. Of course, you will get no sheets let down from heaven in counseling sessions, but you have what is every bit as good – indeed even better since it is complete – the biblical revelation of both the Old and the New Testaments. No one should accept anything less; indeed, no counselor should offer anything less![1]

Finally, we see that, sometime later, Peter had a further problem with this matter – not with understanding, this time, but with following through with that understanding under fear of opposition from others.

> [11]But when Cephas came to Antioch I opposed him to his face because he was obviously wrong. [12]Before certain persons came from James he ate with the Gentiles, but when they came, he withdrew and separated himself, fearing the circumcision party; [13]and the rest of the Jews acted hypocritically with him, so that as a result of their hypocrisy even Barnabas was led astray by them. [14]But when I saw that they weren't walking in line with the truth of the good news, I said to Cephas in front of everybody, "If you, who are a Jew, live like a Gentile and don't live like a Jew, how can you compel Gentiles to live like Jews?" [15]We, who by nature are Jews and not "Gentile sinners," [16]know that a person isn't justified from works of the law but by faith in Christ Jesus. Even we believed in Christ Jesus in order to be justified from faith in Christ and not from works of the law; because nobody will be justified from works of law.
>
> [17]But if while seeking to be justified in Christ we ourselves also were found to be sinners, is Christ then a servant of sin? Of course not! [18]After all, if I build again the same things that I have torn down, then I demonstrate that I myself am a transgressor. [19]I through law died to law so that I might live to God. [20]I have been crucified with Christ, and I no longer live but Christ lives in me. And the life I now live in the flesh I live by

---

1 Why should any counselee accept the best "advice" of another fallible human being? You have something far better; be sure that you use it to the full.

faith from God's Son Who loved me and gave Himself up for me. [21]I will not set aside God's grace; if justification comes by law, then Christ died for nothing (Galatians 2:11–21).

Your counselees may also **revert** to old ways that they know are wrong even after they have ceased resisting, done rethinking, and for a period of time even lived in accordance with the new ways that they have learned. Don't suppose that understanding alone is sufficient. It may take you some time to establish firmly the new ways of God. Don't dismiss the counselee too soon. Rather, plan on getting beyond the turning point to where you are able to root and ground the counselee (Ephesians 3:17) in love for God and for his neighbor. That alone will keep him from reverting in times of temptation and stress.

Moreover, it is important to warn the counselee that such times will come. The problem of over-confidence often arises, as I have mentioned in the previous chapter. There I quoted I Corinthians 10:12, in which Paul warns that it is easy to think that one is able to "stand" when he has not yet had to put his new-found ways to the test. "Pride comes before destruction and a haughty spirit before stumbling" (Proverbs 16:18, NASB). Warn, then, against over-confidence.

Moreover, remind the counselee what to do if and when a fall takes place: "Remember, then, the place from which you have fallen; repent and do the deeds that you did at first" (Revelation 2:5a). Note that the Lord doesn't say that one must "yield," or remember that he isn't an "orphan" and focus on his "adoption," or "preach the gospel to himself again" – all futile methods developed by Christians who have devised their own ways of dealing with temptation, failure, and sin. Rather, the counselor is to urge him under such circumstances to recognize afresh where he went wrong and confess this to God (repent). Then he is to return to his former obedience to God, doing once more "the deeds that he did at first."[1] There could not be a more

---

1 Notice how this verse recognizes that Christians may revert to the former

important warning to give – along with the directions that are set forth by Jesus in Revelation 2:5.

The interesting thing about Peter's case was that he reverted to his old ways – *against* his better knowledge and practice – because of the influence and pressure exerted by other persons (Galatians 2:12–13). In I Corinthians 15:33, Paul warns that "bad companions corrupt good habits." The point he made is that even after good habits have been established, there can be reversion to former ways under the influence of the wrong persons. Throughout Proverbs one's associations are a matter of importance. Here, Peter allowed the men from Jerusalem to influence him more than his knowledge of the Lord's will. To be biblical about it, you will understand that this possibility of reverting exists, and you will anticipate the possibility of it in your conversations with all counselees who have made a break-through. You will warn them especially about the influence or the pressure of other persons upon them. Hardly any other warning could be as important as this one. Your goal is to so root and ground counselees that they are not moved by outside influences. You might also inquire whether there are persons in their venue who would pressure them to give up on their new ways. Warn them and urge them not to listen to those persons but to stick by the Word of God which they have learned.

In all of these ways, you will serve your counselees well, you will serve your Lord, and you will serve the church which needs counselors who do the sorts of things that I have been describing. Are you one? If not, will you become one?

---

ways of sin. But, thankfully, Jesus doesn't leave the matter there. Instead, He shows the way back.

Chapter Eight
Turning Point or Setback?

A turning point becomes a setback when there is inadequate follow-through. I have spoken about some problems (and their sad outcomes evidenced by the counselee) that, following a breakthrough, may either impede progress or lead to his reverting to old, ungodly ways. I have also spoken about the need to recognize and address these before they destroy all of the work that has been done previously. It is time now to mention the equally disastrous effects that may issue from a failure on the part of the counselor to capitalize on the momentum generated when the counselee reaches the turning point. This can be most discouraging to counselees and, if not rectified quickly, may lead to the undoing of his positive accomplishments.

As a matter of fact, when this phenomenon occurs, not only may there be a setback in terms of reversion to old ways but the counselee may become so discouraged after his original enthusiasm has waned, having no appreciable change in his situation, that it may become far more difficult to help him to move ahead in the future. To think that you have made it to a high point where you can see the objective out there in front of you, only to discover that you do not know how to get through the thick and thorny underbrush that lies between you and that objective, can be defeating. You must not allow this to happen to your counselee.

Indeed, at the high point following the breakthrough it is proper to train your sights on the goal that lies ahead. As an incentive, point out to your counselee that he may surely reach this goal by "buckling up the belts" of his mind for "action" (I Peter 1:13). This powerful image makes it clear that the children of God are to be ready to go to work doing those things that please Him. Peter exhorts:

> As children who are under obedience, don't shape your
> lives by the desires that you used to follow in your igno-
> rance. Instead, as the One Who called you is holy, you

yourselves must become holy in all your behavior
(I Peter 1:14–15).

What Peter is calling for is a mindset that is prepared to work.

In contrast to such a mindset, it is possible that both the counselor and the counselee (or either one) may be willing to rest on their laurels. But if the ball is rolling, don't be satisfied with that. Take advantage of your momentum and move counseling farther ahead. All of this I have previously mentioned. But one thing that I have not said is how to move through the underbrush so as to attain the goal. The first thing is for the counselor to congratulate the counselee at the time of the breakthrough: "Well, this is wonderful! God has enabled you to turn an important corner in counseling. Now, from this vantage point you can see where He wants counseling to go next. In order to achieve that goal, you must *set your mind* on attaining it."

So to begin with, the counselor must help the counselee to recognize that the breakthrough isn't the goal. In words and actions he clearly distinguishes the one from the other. Then he makes it clear that the goal (whatever it may be) yet lies ahead. He identifies and sketches it clearly for the counselee. "You have begun to communicate with your wife in a biblical fashion. Good. But there is much to learn about communication under stress, communication that is not monitored by me, communication that brings the two of you together even when you disagree. You are only beginning to understand and practice biblical communication. The goal is to understand and be able to practice communication." Then, the two having agreed upon the goal to be attained, the counselor now urges the counselee to "buckle up his mind for action." That figure of speech comes from the time when men as well as women wore robes. In going to work or to war, you could have become tangled up in your robe if you didn't tuck it up under your girdle or belt. It was an expression similar to our "Roll up your sleeves and get to work." Peter meant that, mentally, you were to prepare yourself to take strenuous "action." Now, there are many who have schemes for attaining the goals that God set forth in the Bible by means other than "action." They want counselees to "trust, yield, abide, preach the gospel again to yourselves" (as I mentioned in the last chapter) or something else. But they do not recommend action. They seem to think that after one puts himself into God's hands (in one way or another) God will do everything from then on. They have prayed – or whatever – so they believe they have punted. The ball is now in God's hands. It is up to Him to carry the ball from this point forward. The key is that they are to be *in*active rather than active. Peter disagrees.

The quietist (one who thinks that way) fails to see that the choice is not an either/or choice. It is not a matter of God or the Christian bringing about the sanctifying results that are desired. No, throughout the Bible it is clear that sanctification is a both/ and situation. It is not God alone or man alone who sanctifies. It is God giving the wisdom, direction, and strength to enable the Christian to do those things that He has required of him.

For Christians to take action – rather than to follow their former "desires" – must *not* be considered self-righteousness or legalism, as these "quietists" often call action. We see that according to Ephesians 2:10, God considers the believer *His* "handiwork." That certainly is true. But what is this handiwork of His like? Is it an inanimate object to be driven about by His Spirit? Is it a robot? Or a piece of plastic to be shaped? No. It is a living, responsible human being who must sustain a relationship of love to Him and to his neighbor. That requires attitudes and actions on the part of the Christian that are worked in him by God (Philippians 2:12–13). This work of the Spirit in the believer *enables him to do those things that please Him.* According to Ephesians 2:10, mentioned above, the handiwork of God – the Christian – is "created in Christ Jesus *for* good works." In other words, for *action.* Paul and Peter agree. Both disagree with the quietist.

So the believer is responsible for calling on God for direction and for help, but also for doing something about the direction, with the power that the Spirit provides through His Word. Here's how Peter goes on to describe the action that a child of God is to pursue:

[13] Therefore, buckling the belts of your minds for action, keeping level-headed, set your hope entirely on the grace that will be brought to you at the revelation of Jesus Christ. [14] As children who are under obedience, don't shape your lives by the desires that you used to follow in your ignorance. [15] Instead, as the One Who called you is holy, you yourselves must become holy in all your behavior. [16] I say this because it is written: "You must be holy because I am holy."

[17] If you call Him Father Who impartially judges each one by his deeds, then be deeply concerned about how you behave during your residence as aliens, [18] knowing that you weren't set free from the useless behavior patterns that were passed down from your forefathers by the payment of a corruptible ransom like silver or gold, [19] but with Christ's valuable blood, shed like the blood of a spotless and unblemished lamb. [20] He was foreknown, indeed, before the foundation of a world, but at these last times He made His appearance for your sake [21] who through Him have believed in God, Who raised Him from the dead and gave Him glory, so that your faith and hope are in God.

[22] Having cleansed yourselves by obedience to the truth you can have brotherly affection without pretense; so love one another intensively from the heart, [23] having been regenerated not by perishable seed, but by that which is imperishable – God's living and continuing Word. [24] Do this because "all flesh is like grass and all its glory is like a flower of grass: The grass withered and the flower fell off, [25] but the Lord's Word remains forever."

Now, this is the Word that was announced to you as good news. [1] Therefore, having put off all malice, and all pretense and hypocritical ways, and envious attitudes, and all evil speaking about others, [2] like newborn babies, crave pure milk from the Word so that by it you may grow toward salvation, [3] since you have tasted that the Lord is good (I Peter 1:13–2:3).

From this extended passage you can easily discern the following:

1. Believers are to have minds set for strenuous action for God.
2. They are to take action according to His Word.
3. This action is to be taken *in contrast to* following one's former sinful desires.
4. This is possible because Jesus has set us free from following past behavior patterns.
5. The ultimate goal is the glorifying grace that will be given at Christ's revelation.
6. Intermediate goals (like those in counseling) are reached by reshaping the life now.
7. This is achieved by adopting holy (set apart according to Scripture) behavior.
8. The believer does this to please God, Who is greatly concerned about his behavior.
9. Obedient children seek to conform to the truth in God's Word.
10. God's Word shows them what sins to put off and what righteous behavior to put on instead.

So, counselor, your task is to encourage the breakthrough believer to begin to become rooted in love so that he will not be shaken by temptation or adversity. This is done by Spirit-directed and -strengthened action on his part as an obedient child who wishes to please his heavenly Father. Obedience is the key word in the passage. It is obedient action to which Peter calls his reader. It is not some sort of inaction like "remembering," "resting," or "abiding."[1] This obedient action is exactly that to which the counselor must call his counselee as well. He must represent the great divide over which he has come as only the prelude to vigorous action in rooting himself by God's grace

---

1 The passage from which the quietistic notion of "abiding" comes is John 15. There, Jesus makes it clear that the Christian must abide in Him. But this is a verse that speaks primarily of perseverance, not sanctification. To "abide" means, literally, "to remain." If one does not "remain" (or stay) in the Vine

in the new ways. This is the goal that lies before him.

How does the counselor proceed? By calling the counselee to become rehabituated in God's new ways. (For details on this, see my book *The Christian Counselor's Manual* where the put off/put on dynamic of the Bible is discussed thoroughly. See also my *Winning the War Within*, which is largely an exposition and discussion of Romans 6 and 7 with reference to the difficulties that may be encountered in the process). This rehabituation of the body is a very significant part of establishing him in the new ways. Because learning all new habits takes time, the counselor will not allow the counselee to think that since he made the breakthrough, he has "arrived." No, in one sense he has but begun the journey! That is the attitude and the stance that the counselor should take when addressing the question, "Where do we go from here?"

The counselor is interested in seeing rapid progress now, progress no longer impeded by sin, ignorance, disobedience, and the like. In one sense, he should be rubbing his hands, saying, "Ah! Now at last we can begin to see some real progress!" If a counselor is conscientious about doing this, he will find that his counselee, having newly crossed the divide, is likely to become enthusiastic about going ahead (producing fruit, as Jesus put it). He will neither lag behind nor want to quit counseling too soon. And these are precisely the problems that you want to avoid at this stage. So plan to make much of the possibilities over the other side of the hump! This is the time when – of all times – the counselee should be pliable and willing to hear you and to move ahead with alacrity. Don't miss the opportunity!

(Jesus) he can "do nothing" (v. 5). By staying in the vine (i.e., demonstrating that one's faith is genuine) one can produce much fruit. It is obviously no quietistic notion to "do" and to "produce fruit" by "keeping" Christ's "commandments" (v. 10). The passage is quite activistic, in every good sense of that word. The power comes from the Vine, but the fruit is produced by the branches. The coupling of divine and human action is, as always, found even in this supposedly pivotal quietistic passage! For more on the matter of the relation of the divine and the human, see *Maintaining the Delicate Balance in Christian Living.*

Chapter Nine

The Heart Issue

In the last chapter I emphasized the importance of taking action after a breakthrough. Now I want to talk about the motivation behind action. It is not enough to outwardly "do" what God requires; there must always be a proper heart attitude behind what one does. Otherwise, the action is *not* what God requires. It is legalistic to think that the rich young ruler was right when he declared that from his youth up he had kept all the commandments. In examining that story, it should become apparent that Christ was saying there was heart failure!

> [18] Then a certain ruler questioned Him, saying, "Good teacher, what shall I do to inherit eternal life?" [19] Jesus replied, "Why do you call Me good? Nobody is good except God Himself. [20] You know the commandments – 'Do not commit adultery, Do not kill, Do not steal, Do not bear false witness, Honor your father and mother.'" [21] Then he said, "I have kept them all since I was a boy." [22] When Jesus heard this, He said to him, "You still lack one thing. Sell everything you have, give the money to the poor, and you will have treasure in heaven. Then come, follow Me." [23] But when he heard this, he became quite upset, because he was very rich. [24] When Jesus saw his reaction, He said, "How hard it is for those who have riches to enter God's empire! [25] It is easier for a camel to go through the eye of a needle than for a rich man to enter God's empire." (Luke 18:18-25)

There are a number of facts to discern in this story, all of which relate to the point of this chapter. Note several:

1. The rich man had "kept" God's commandments (outwardly) from his youth up (v. 21). There is no reason to doubt this. Jesus does not challenge the statement.
2. He thought that Jesus was a "good" man and called Him such (v. 18).

3. Jesus refused to accept this designation of Himself. Why? Wasn't He good? Yes, of course. But we shall see why He refused.
4. Jesus said that only God was "good" (v. 19).
5. Jesus said that the man lacked but one thing (v. 22). What was this? It was demonstrated by the failure of the ruler to agree to the homework assignments that Christ gave him.
6. Those assignments were: first, to sell all he had and give the money received to the poor; second, to come follow Him.
7. The rich ruler was quite upset at what Jesus required of him (v. 23).

Now, what shall we make of all of this?

Look first at the word "good." Why does Jesus reject the ruler's evaluation of himself as such? Because the ruler's evaluation was incorrect. Indeed, Jesus corrects him (v. 19). He thought that to be good meant to conform to the commandments *outwardly*. When he applied the term to Jesus, therefore, he thought also of Him that way. He classified Jesus in a category with himself! He had no idea that Jesus was God and that only a perfect God-man in this sinful world could fulfill the commandments. Unless he was prepared to call Jesus "God," therefore, he should not call him good (cf. Romans 3:10, 3:23).

But the one thing that the ruler lacked was this: he had not kept the commandments *in his heart*. While he had never killed a man, he had hated in his heart; while he had never committed adultery, he had done so in his heart. He lacked an understanding of how God viewed the commandments. He lacked the love that keeping the two great commandments demonstrates. These two comprehensive commandments were to love God and to love one's neighbor. Jesus said that on the two love commandments hang all the law and the prophets.

"How do we know that it was this inner love that was lacking?" you may ask. Because that is precisely what the rich young ruler demonstrated by his refusal that he lacked. He would not show love either to his neighbor or to God. Jesus' two assignments were not calculated to be assignments for all counselees. They were specifically designed to expose this ruler's lack of love. To give his riches to the poor, and to follow Jesus in poverty, was something he was not prepared to do under any condition – even to "inherit eternal life." Not that such "works" would bring him eternal life, but they would demonstrate that in his heart there was a genuine disposition to keep the two great commandments – a disposition that grows out of salvation.

It is important to note that all those who think that they are pleasing God by keeping counseling assignments must be told to obey from the heart. It is not enough to line up the required actions and then do them *seriatim*. Neither is there merit in that alone, as some think. Rather, those who think that there is have the mind of the Pharisee at work within them. The Pharisee, Jesus said, washed the outside of the cup, but inside it was full of corruption. The Pharisee, He continued, was like a whitewashed grave that looked good on the outside, but was full of death and corruption within. The Pharisee vainly tried to earn acceptance and approval by God through these outer works. In short, there must be reality, love, faith, and genuineness within, as well as proper action without.

I have been accused of teaching behaviorism because in some of my earlier writings I did not explain this thoroughly enough. Wrongly, I expected the reader to know that when I spoke from the Bible about "action," I meant the one and only kind that God accepts – works motivated by faith and love. But some did not understand. Here, I want to make it explicit that the sort of action that Peter and I are talking about[1] is action that not only conforms outwardly to God's commands, but conforms inwardly as well. It was that inner conformity that the ruler lacked. This was demonstrated, I noted, by his failure to take Christ up on His homework assignments.

So, too, the counselee who wants only to comply outwardly will fail to do those things that demonstrate that his heart is right before God and before men.[2] He too may become disturbed

---

1 See the previous chapter.
2 The biblical concept of "heart" differs from the modern Western view. To us, heart usually describes emotion or feeling ("I love you with all my

when you show him what God expects from him. There is no way that you can know another's heart. But you can do two things to help the counselee to consider his. First, you can make a point of the fact that he must obey "from the heart" (Romans 6:17). You can warn about the temptation to merely conform outwardly and mention the hard words that Jesus had for the Pharisees who did so, calling them snakes and hypocrites!

Then, secondly, you can give some assignments that may indicate to the counselee whether or not he is genuine, as Jesus did with the ruler. What might such an assignment look like? Take the following example: Here is a man who says that he wants to give up the pornography that he has been looking at on the Internet and on the TV. Ask him, if he is earnest about changing, to sell his TV and his computer and give the proceeds to the church. Then, during the time that he has been devoting to sinful viewing, call him rather to devote himself to Bible study. There is no way that he will even contemplate doing so if he is not genuine. His feathers will be ruffled at the suggestion. Of course, you cannot compel him to do this, as if the specifics were a divine command, but both you and he can get some indication of his sincerity by posing the possibility. Each homework assignment ought to be designed to meet the specific situation, just as Jesus' was.

How can a man know his own heart? Granted, there is so much evil and deception we are capable of that we may have

---

heart!"). We distinguish between head (intellect) and heart (emotion): "What we need is less head knowledge and more heart knowledge." The Bible never makes this disjunction: the intellect is *included* in "heart" (cf. Hebrews 4:12). "Heart," in the Bible, is contrasted with mouth, lips, hands and "outward appearance" (I Samuel 16:7). What it refers to, as Peter put it, is "the *hidden person* of the heart," the inner you (I Peter 3:4). It means the inner, genuine you; not the "you" that you project to others. It includes conscience and the reasoning (and other self-talk) that goes on within. It is the part of you known only to God in the full sense of the term "know." Others can get a glimpse of what is in the heart by what comes from the mouth and what flows into the outer actions (Proverbs 4:23). Yet these judgments from words and actions (the only ones we are allowed to make) are always only approximate, and may be far from the mark.

difficulty here. So the assignment that you give him – or one he devises along the same lines – may help. But, of course, as you (or he) design assignments, you must be careful to make it clear that the assignment holds no merit (people will want to fulfill them for this wrong reason), as I made clear in my exposition of Luke 18 above. Rather, the reasons for the assignment are to test one's own heart and to do the good to others that a person has been refraining from doing (possibly) from his youth up! To love one's neighbor and to love God was the need of the ruler. Attempt to discern any such lack in your counselee by designing his exposing homework assignments accordingly.

It is wonderful to have a clear conscience in these matters (not one seared by a hot iron[1]). But if your counselee genuinely believes that he has love for God and neighbor in what he is doing in order to reach the goal, yet has a nagging conscience, he can only go so far. He must do all that he can to maintain a clear conscience, searching his heart. But if his heart still condemns him, he must leave the matter to God, Who is greater than the heart, and then proceed to do what God commands (cf. I John 3:19–21). He must not be hindered from doing what Scripture outlines for him by such suspicions. Rather, he must say with the apostle Paul, "I don't even judge myself" (I Corinthians 4:3; see vv. 1–5). He leaves the judgment to the Lord (v. 4).

One additional test (to be used with great care) is mentioned in II Corinthians 8:8, where Paul discusses giving for the poor saints at Jerusalem. He says, "I am testing the reality of your love by comparing it with the eagerness of others." Comparisons – except with regard to the demonstration of love by works – are dangerous. But an astute counselor like Paul would have had enough experience to ascertain something about whether there was genuine love for the poor by what the Corinthians gave in comparison to others of like means and situation. And,

---

1 Both a clear and a seared conscience will mean that there is no condemnation, but for opposite reasons!

138

indeed, he does this very thing in the letter, concluding that they were in earnest.

In one way or another – while not transgressing the limits God has placed on us in knowing another's heart (remember, *He* is the Heart-Knower)[1] – it is important to do all that you can to be sure the counselee takes action from the heart. The heart and the hands, the heart and the mouth must be in sync. Certainly, that was always true only of One Other – the Lord Jesus Christ of Whom, alone, it could be said that He was "good" in the absolute sense of the word. Others, in this life, will have to settle for a growing goodness as they grow into His likeness. But they will become fully like Him only when they see Him as He is in His glorified humanity, and are transformed perfectly into His likeness.

---

1 Your judgment, as well as your counselee's, will always be tentative, and often faulty.

Chapter Ten

Referring

Sometimes you will counsel someone from another congregation. This calls for certain considerations that would not otherwise concern you. Many times problems arise unnecessarily from such a situation. I will try to address how to avoid some of the more prominent ones.

The first consideration concerns *how* you accept referrals from another church and *when* you will accept persons wandering from other fellowships who desire counseling from you. Consider the latter first. There are many people who do not want to go to their own pastor for counseling for various reasons. One is to avoid embarrassment, to avoid revealing sordid details, and so on. Another reason is because the person does not think that his pastor has the ability to counsel him well. A third is that he has had a bad experience with a pastor (either the present or a past one). Leaking details about a counselee's case is a frequent complaint. There are, of course, many more possibilities, but these are the most common.

To avoid either embarrassment or revealing data to one's pastor are illegitimate reasons. Here is a person who needs to be taught that the task of a shepherd (the word "pastor" means "shepherd") is to care for the sheep in all their needs[1] (cf. Jeremiah 23:1–4). This wandering sheep who arrives at your church door should be exhorted (perhaps in an initial exploratory session) to go back to his pastor for counseling, or to ask his pastor to accompany him, and sit in on counseling under you. But, in

---

1 See also Psalm 23, "The Lord is my Shepherd [pastor]; I shall not lack." This statement is an enthymeme (i.e., a syllogism in which one of the three propositions is assumed rather than stated). It runs like this:
The Lord is my Shepherd
[True Shepherds meet all the needs of their sheep]
Therefore, I shall lack no care that I need.

all such cases, it is imperative to try to involve his pastor in a proper and vital way.

But what if the potential counselee says that he doesn't want to destroy the good relationship that he has with his pastor by letting him know about his sins and weaknesses, as many do? He has come to you for anonymity. You must answer that in the Bible the sheep are drawn closer to their pastor and the good shepherd to his sheep by facing problems, trials and the like *together* (cf. John 10). He knows them individually – by name – with all their quirks and eccentricities, and they will not follow the voice of another shepherd. There is something wrong with the sheep who *thinks* that he has a close relationship to his shepherd (pastor) yet wanders afield in search of another counselor. Perhaps he needs to develop a different sort of relationship to his shepherd – one that is much deeper – as a result of facing the present trial together. Urge him (even help him by phone calls, meetings with the three of you, etc.) to bring this matter to his pastor.

But there are those other situations where the pastor is not a competent counselor. He may even admit this to his people, or to this counselee. If he doesn't in so many words, he may say something like "I don't do counseling," "I think that if you study these five verses and pray about them, God will help you to work out your problem," or words to the same effect. Your counselee may know that he needs more than what that pastor may be able or willing to give. Perhaps he is a young man, fresh out of seminary, just learning. Possibly he is older but was never trained in biblical counseling. It is quite likely that he may be one who refers his counselees to psychologists or to eclectic "Christian counselors." Instead, rightly, your potential counselee may want someone who will counsel him biblically.

In all such cases, you will want to persuade him (again, possibly in a preliminary, exploratory session) to involve his pastor. You should extend an offer to have his pastor "sit in" on sessions. Often, this will be threatening to pastors whose pride will not allow them to do so. But that is something that you will have to contend with as well. You simply explain to the would-be counselee that it is your policy, from which you do not depart, to have his pastor (or, at the very least, an elder of his congregation) present for all sessions. You should explain that you simply do not advise counselees apart from their pastor knowing what it is that you are counseling them to believe and to do. Tell him that you are concerned not to imperil the integrity of the shepherd/sheep relationship that they share. He may then inform his pastor about these things.

If the pastor of your potential counselee does not know how to counsel, he will have an opportunity to learn something from the sessions. Actually, when it becomes known that you counsel effectively, some pastors may even begin to *send* counseling cases to you instead of doing the counseling themselves. These men need to be brought into counseling sessions to assume at least part of their responsibility for their sheep – regardless of the reason they refer rather than counsel themselves. If they are lazy, perhaps you can help them along the way to change. If they are incompetent, but willing to learn, there are few better ways to equip them than by allowing them to "sit in" on your counseling. This is one method by which we have successfully trained many pastors and counselors over the years.

Moreover – and this involves you most directly during the post-breakthrough period – when the pastor is present in your sessions, at some juncture during this period you may be able to "hand over" the counselee (with appropriate instructions) to his pastor to complete the counseling case. This will save you much valuable time, and will allow you to focus on your own members more faithfully. And it will help the counselee's pastor "save face." It is this aspect of the matter of referral to which I want to address myself most fully in what follows.

But, first, there are other situations. There are cases in which counselees' pastors will not come – or, in which you do not want them to come! Consider the latter. The potential counselee may belong to a liberal congregation or denomination. In such cases, the pastor may be a wolf in shepherd's clothing rather than a shepherd. Your task may be to tell the counselee from the outset (perhaps during a preliminary session or two) that you will also counsel him to leave his church and join a Bible-believing one like yours[1] (of course!). His church may not be liberal, but may refuse to do church discipline, yet that is precisely what a given case calls for. You may attempt to get the church to act biblically in this matter, but their refusal may lead to the advice to leave and join a church that does practice discipline in a biblical manner.[2] Sadly, many other reasons might be advanced that would lead to such advice. But in contrast – and this is quite important – where there is a good shepherd who will accompany his sheep to counseling, you must do all that you can to preserve and enrich the shepherd/sheep relationship. You may not use counseling as a means of stealing sheep from such a shepherd. By all means "free" sheep from the clutches of bad shepherds and those who prove to be wolves who devour the flock. But be absolutely sure of your facts before you attempt to do so.

What of the situation mentioned above, in which a pastor has accompanied his sheep to your counseling sessions which have now reached the turning point? Here is where you are required to exercise wisdom. During the counseling sessions (and possibly afterward, when you and his pastor meet together to discuss the case) you have been evaluating how well the pastor has learned from the counseling. You have brought him actively into the case, asking for his comments from time to time, and you see that they are right on the mark. This man is growing. So you have not only been counseling the counselee;

---

1 The presupposition here is that he is a genuine believer who is the member of a wrong congregation. This fact may emerge in the first session from data on the PDI (see page 22 in *Getting Started* for details on the PDI), or from discussion with the counselee. He may say, for instance, that his pastor advises divorce, in what you know, biblically, is a non-divorce situation. A discussion of this may bring out the fact of liberal teaching. On the other hand, there are certain denominations, or congregations, that you know from the outset are liberal.

2 See my *Handbook of Church Discipline*, especially the chapter on interchurch discipline.

you have also been carefully watching his pastor.[1]

If you determine that the pastor is able to carry the counseling from that point[2] to the finish, you will be glad to help him do so. Laying out a plan for the next six weeks (or whatever you estimate the remainder of the counseling may take), you tell the counselee, "We have gotten over the hump, and I am sure that you and your pastor can carry on without me from here on." This plan should be written out, explained, and agreed upon by all concerned. It is important that *everyone* knows what everyone knows, and that *all* know that all know it. In this way, neither the pastor nor the counselee is likely to shirk the work yet to be done. But that does not mean that you may not want to sit down with the pastor privately to make sure that he knows what to do. In addition, you may want to let him know that you will be available for telephone consultation with him, that you would be willing to have him bring his counselee back at any time they get stuck, and that in all cases, you'd like to have a future, final visit with him and his counselee(s) when he believes that counseling should be terminated.

These precautionary measures are designed to help the pastor by structuring what he will do from that point on. They also call him and the counselee to responsibility. And they provide a safety net for all involved. Consider another fact. Unwittingly, you may actually have begun to provide counseling training for pastors in your community by means of this approach. This same pastor, intrigued by what has happened, having grown close to you and wanting to learn more, may wish to sit in on other cases of yours. Indeed, if you think that it is appropriate to do so, and he doesn't ask, you may even offer for him to do it. In time, the word may get out and other pastors in town may want to do the same, bringing some of their harder cases to you. Establishing such a training program may lead to great blessing

---

1 Some pastors will not grow appreciably. In such cases, wisdom must be exercised to discover why and to determine what action you should take.
2 Usually, this will be no sooner than a week or two after the breakthrough, wait to be sure that the change is sufficient and is likely to last.

in the area, and to many more pastors assuming their shepherdly responsibilities. Consider it seriously.[1]

So the important fact to remember here is that referral to you should always be referral by the pastor of his counselee *and of himself.* There may be times when *you* need to refer a counselee to another trusted pastor. When this occurs, ask for permission to sit in so that you will learn more. Otherwise, you will be as ignorant at the end as you were at the beginning. And – of greater import – you will have missed the opportunity to show your sheep that you care enough to accompany him to counseling.

---

1 In time, you may wish to set up a training program in a more formal manner, actually offering courses of study and discussion along with the opportunity to sit in on cases brought by pastors. A maximum number of counselors (pastors) sitting in on any one case ought to be two. Be sure that you spend time discussing sessions afterwards. If more than two pastors are taking training at the same time, you may have them report on cases in which they are participating to the others, who are sitting in on different cases (about which they too will report to the group). In this way a lot of experience may be gained in a minimum of time.

Chapter Eleven

Picking Up the Pieces

Frequently, the turning point in counseling is a true *break*-through, which involves the breaking up of previous relationships, patterns of living, and the like. Jesus demands radical change that is equivalent to a destruction of much of the past. The counselor must be prepared to warn the counselee that change may be a shattering experience. When Jesus begins to reorient our lives He shakes things up (cf. Ephesians 4:17); there must be a clear disjunction between our past and our future lives. In calling Jeremiah, God put it this way: "I have appointed you...to root up, to break down, to destroy, to exterminate, to rebuild and to establish" (Jeremiah 1:10, *Berkeley*).

But you will notice in the above quotation, I hope, that while much must be destroyed in making things right with God, there must be a positive component as well: Jeremiah was ordered not only to break down, but also to "rebuild" and "establish." What is demolished must be replaced by its biblical alternative. The same must take place in counseling as well; if it doesn't, the counselee will tend to drift into his old ways, or new sinful ways, because, as in nature, persons abhor a vacuum. In a world of sin, that means that something *wrong* will fill the empty space; one never drifts toward that which is right. On the new side of the turning point, your counselees must form and build new relationships and new lifestyles that grow out of new thoughts and attitudes, new decisions and commitments.

The sort of new life with which a counselee emerges from counseling will depend in large measure upon how well you are able to help him to pick up the pieces of his life and rearrange them according to a biblical blueprint. To the extent that he may fail to do so, the breakthrough is likely to be useless – or what is worse, positively harmful! He may revert to old, sinful thoughts and behaviors or develop new ones that will continue to dishonor God and destroy his life in other ways. All the time and effort expended in counseling will have been expended in vain. There are few things more disheartening than for a counselee to reach a high point at one moment, only to be let down hard shortly thereafter.

While the parable of the house swept clean has to do with Israel's rejection of the gospel (Matthew 12:43–45), which only led to greater and more serious apostasy, the principle underlying the parable applies to how all evil operates – whether found in the apostasy of a nation, the life of a pagan, or in the experience of a believer. It is this: failure to replace that which is wrong with that which is right leads to an even more serious condition.

As I have mentioned elsewhere, God assures us in Isaiah 55 that His ways are not our ways and that His thoughts are not our thoughts. In that place He also declared that His ways and thoughts are "higher" than ours. When old ways and thoughts are smashed at the breakthrough, they must be *replaced* by God's new, higher ones. That means that in various aspects of his life, the counselee must be shown what the higher ways of God are and how to attain to them. If he fails to exhibit a higher sort of life in days and months following the turning point, something was seriously wrong with post-breakthrough counseling. Now, let's think about some ways in which the swept house may be reoccupied so as to bring it more under God's sway.

Old associations may have to be modified. I have noted that, as Paul says in I Corinthians 15:33, wrong relationships may be harmful and may undo all the good done in counseling. Homosexual and heterosexual alliances must be severed. And there can be no lingering about it. The break in the relationship should be clean; no ragged edges may be countenanced.

I can hear the protest that will arise when you tell that to your counselee: "But now that I have repented of the sin with Joe, and found forgiveness in Christ, I want to help him to do the same." But you must respond by saying something like "You are too weak at this point to do so. You must have nothing more to do with him." Instead, you may have to help your counselee to enlist a pastor or some other mature Christian to speak to the estranged person about Christ. Otherwise he runs the danger of allowing him to "corrupt" the new ways on which he has so recently embarked.

The house will not remain unoccupied. The question in the post-breakthrough period is "Who will move in?" Assure your counselees that unless they are careful to choose the right new occupants they may be certain that the wrong ones will soon arrive and begin unpacking their luggage. But they must not only guard against wrong occupants, they must carefully select the right ones. In this respect, picking up the pieces means orienting one's Bible-shattered, sinful lifestyle toward establishing and building firm relationships with other believers whose lives will be an example of godly living and who will also encourage counselees in God's higher ways.

Warn your counselees about these dangers, counsel them to pursue godly friends and associates, and monitor their progress in the matter. If progress is slow, or if the counselee has difficulty making new friends, you may have to become rather fully involved:

1. You may have to teach something of the art of making friends.

2. You may have to help enlist potential friends – or get help from those who can – from among the members of his church.

3. You may find it necessary to aid, assist and direct the counselee in overcoming obstacles in developing godly friendships.

As you prepare the counselee for future successes in living for God, few issues are as important as this matter of developing godly relationships.

Different life patterns that conform to Scripture must replace old, sinful ones. Consider **patterns of the thought life**. In a seminal discussion of overcoming worry (which is essential to peaceful, Christian living), Paul sets forth a set of criteria by which the thought life may be evaluated. He wrote:

Finally, brothers, whatever is true, whatever is serious, whatever is just, whatever is pure, whatever is lovely, whatever is of good repute, if there is anything morally excellent, and if there is anything praiseworthy, focus your thinking on these things (Philippians 4:8).

You must teach your counselee to so discipline his mind that instead of drifting into worry, sordid sexual fantasies, or bitter and evil intentions, it will learn to reject these whenever they arise in favor of the "excellent" things that fit the categories found in verse 8.[1]

Concern about **behavior** did not begin with Skinner (or John Watson). God regularly speaks about the matter in the Scriptures. Behavior, which grows out of the heart, must be restructured. The change begins with the heart but must extend to actions. When God speaks of conforming our "thoughts" and our "ways" to His by His Word, He makes it clear that both must change. Change of heart, which includes the thought life (see Hebrews 4:12), does not automatically lead to changes in behavior. Some oppose directing others to *do* anything about their outward lifestyle on the basis that it is the Spirit's work to change their behavior. But it is no more the Spirit's work to change their heart than to change their behavior. The Spirit works in both the inner and the outer dimensions.

Whenever a believer abandons ungodly practices and replaces them with godly ones, both the putting off of the former and the putting on of the latter is ultimately the work of the Holy Spirit. He inspired the Bible (which is the Standard by which our lives are to be governed), He enlightens us to understand and assimilate scriptural teaching, He urges and enables us to pray that God may bless our efforts to conform to the Bible, and He encourages and strengthens us by that Word to do as it directs. But it is not *He*, it is *we* who must "observe" the things that He has commanded us (Matthew 28:20).

---

1 For more about worry, together with a discussion of Matthew 6, see my book *The Christian Counselor's Manual* and the pamphlet *What to Do When you Worry All the Time.*

Some counselors have too high a view of the place of education. They think that if they instruct their people well, they will respond well by putting their teaching into practice. That notion is patently untrue. There are all sorts of scriptural teachings that every Christian knows he ought to do, but he continually fails to do them. He knows much of what he ought not to do, but does it anyway. Though freed from slavery from his past sinful ways (cf. I Peter 1:18ff., Romans 6), and freed to do righteousness instead, we must still be urged to live by those truths which we have learned (cf. Philippians 3:16). None of us lives up to his knowledge of God's will. This fact is pertinent especially to the post-breakthrough counselee who needs instruction, encouragement, and help in refashioning his shattered lifestyle to conform to biblical ways. The turning point will fail to be a true turning point if, instead of a 180° turn, he makes a 360° turn instead. Your task is to see that he does not turn back to old ways of which he has repented, and to assist him in turning to God's, new righteous ways. This can be done only by restructuring your counselee's lifestyle according to biblical patterns of thought and action. Make sure that you are aware of this fact and follow through on the far side of the breakthrough.

Chapter Twelve
Taking Care

I have mentioned "ministering" the Scriptures to counselees. There is a large difference between ministering and "prescribing" Scripture. By "prescribing," I mean doling out Bible verses much as a doctor hands out prescriptions: "Take these verses three times a day with prayer." That is *not* ministering the Word. Don't ever become a Bible-dispensing machine! To hand out Bible verses in that manner, naturally, is superior to doing nothing or ignoring Scripture as many do. The Spirit, Who has determined to work through His Word, may indeed use those verses in spite of the fact that the "counselor" does little more than dispense them. He is not limited by human agency. But, according to many passages, those who use the Bible are strongly encouraged to do far more. They are commanded to "exhort, urge, persuade, teach,[1] apply, rebuke and convict" by the Word (cf. II Timothy 4:2, etc.).

The Spirit also *expects* those who use His Word to minister it "accurately" (II Timothy 2:15). Obviously, this requires faithfulness and skill on the counselor's part and a great deal of humble learning on the part of the counselees. Counselors must select biblical portions wisely, those that pertain directly or indirectly to the counselee and his situation, applying them to both along with proper interpretation and implementation so as to help the counselee put them into practice. Passages will refer to intellectual, attitudinal, and behavioral aspects of the counselee's life. All must be included. Since all of these factors are necessary, let us consider them in logical sequence.

There are four steps to ministering the Word in sessions and in homework. They may be easily remembered by a simple acrostic: C-A-R-E. The Word is properly ministered[2] when passages are

---

1 See my book *Teaching to Observe*.
2 The Word, like meals, must be ministered or "served" (cf. Acts 6:2–4). The

Carefully selected,
Accurately interpreted,
Rigorously applied,
Effectively implemented.

Careful selection of scriptural passages is the first step. Unless the counselor possesses a reservoir of well-known passages that pertain to various situations on which he may draw, he will tend to rely on too few. Difficulties into which human beings may get themselves, or that others may foist upon them, are vast and varied. That means that the counselor must continually expand his knowledge of Scripture – something that many fail to do. The almost right passage may at times do, and God may bless its use during one's early counseling days, but it rarely is as effective as the passage that precisely fits the counseling problem. And without a wide knowledge of Scripture, a counselor will tend to use passages for purposes they were never intended to serve. At worst, he may distort and misapply Scripture so as to make God say things that He never did.

A preacher knows beforehand what verse or verses he will preach from. He can study, ponder, and interpret his preaching portion for quite some time prior to the delivery of his sermon. The counselor has no such luxury; he never knows for certain where counseling may lead in any given session and, consequently, what passages of Scripture he may need to minister. Unsuspected facts or problems may emerge at any time. That is why his knowledge and understanding of the Bible must be broad. He must be able to draw from much careful and current exegetical and doctrinal study.[1]

---

same Greek word is used in this passage in contrast for both: serving tables and serving the Word.

1 One reason why counseling is best done by pastors is that they must study the Scriptures daily in order to prepare for sermons. Many who only counsel do not do daily, intensive study of the sort needed. Rather, if they read at all, they spend their time reading the latest counseling books. Pastors are disciplined by the weekly preaching task to study the Bible.

While this need for a wide-ranging knowledge of Scripture may be supplied in many ways as a counselor's grasp of the Scriptures is growing in undisciplined and irregular ways, I recommend regular, disciplined study. A good place to begin is with the topical list of passages in the back of the *Christian Counselor's New Testament*. In the back of that volume, there is also an index of marginal notations designed to help the counselor quickly find key passages on various topics. What he might do is go through these passages systematically each week, exegeting them with the help of commentaries until he is familiar enough with the location, meaning, and purpose of each. That sort of study is essential for one to obtain the wide working knowledge of Scripture from which he may select the passages required to meet any counseling situation. Careful selection, then, necessitates a large pool of known passages and requires the counselor's thorough understanding of each. I shall not say more than to note here that even with a wide knowledge of Scripture, one must acquire wisdom to know which to use in which situation.[1]

While careful selection is important at all stages of counseling, it is especially important for the post-breakthrough period. During the pre-breakthrough time, passages concerning sin, rebellion, confession and repentance, and the like, along with those that have to do with hope and encouragement, probably will predominate. You will probably need fewer at this point than later on when rebuilding the counselee's life, since many of the former passages will pertain to most cases. In the post-breakthrough period, however, the "put on" passages – those according to which the counselor directs the counselee in picking up the pieces and rebuilding his life patterns – are likely to be more varied. The tearing down of a building may demand less ingenuity and thought than the design and erection of a new one. Dynamite and bulldozers alone may carry out the first task effectively, whereas it will take architects, bricklayers, carpen-

---

1 See my book *A Call for Discernment* for more on acquiring discernment and wisdom.

ters, plumbers, roofers, and electricians to bring the latter to completion. That is why I have included a chapter concerning such matters in the second book of this trilogy. I commend to you, therefore, a serious study of the passages topically listed to which I referred so that the locations, meanings, and purposes of each will be at your fingertips at all times.

Accurate interpretation is the second element. Out of concern about how the Word of God is ministered, Paul wrote, "Do your best to present yourself to God tried and true, a workman who won't be ashamed, handling the Word of truth with accuracy" (II Timothy 2:15). Notice the phrase "handling...with accuracy" (literally, "cutting straight"). To be a workman in the Word who will have no reason to be "ashamed" of his shoddy work demands accuracy and precision in interpreting the Scriptures. That's what "cutting straight" is all about. He must "do his best" to understand and express its true and full meaning to each counselee.

Some counselors will be ashamed, not only before men (even some counselees may catch them on their faulty interpretations), but also as they stand before God some day. Of course, one cannot know everything about the Bible at once. God takes this into account when He calls us to constant "progress" (*proskope*).[1] Any counseling that is not better this year than it was last year clearly demonstrates that something is wrong. The counselor has not been growing as he ought – and that may be principally because of his failure to do serious Bible study in conjunction with his counseling. Indeed, progress ought to be so conspicuous that those who observe can readily detect it: it should be "apparent to everybody" (I Timothy 4:15). I urge you to stock up on good Bible reference books and commentaries – and to use them!

Rigorous application is the third step. A dangerous movement is afoot in some circles today in which preachers and counselors are cautioned *against* applying the Bible – and cen-

---

1 The word used in I Timothy 4:15 means entering new territory, blazing a trail in virgin territory.

sured for doing it! This extremist position is akin to that sort of Lutheranism that denied the third use of the law (i.e., as a guide for Christian living). I have mentioned this movement in a previous chapter in regard to its quietistic[1] outworkings. The Spirit alone is expected to apply the Scriptures to individuals. Quite contrary to the express teaching of Scripture itself, the movement condemns application (exhortation, persuasion, urging, rebuke, etc.) as "legalistic" or as "works righteousness." The fact is, this unbiblical approach is antinomian in nature.[2]

Those churches that followed the Lutheran tradition have not been known for changing people's lives appreciably. Unfortunately, their pietistic, quietistic, antinomian emphases have lately been invading even Calvinistic churches. This is in contrast to the Westminster standards on sanctification by which they are governed!

When it comes to counseling, Scripture must be rigorously applied to counselees. What do I mean by that? I am saying that, without becoming rude or crude, you must set forth God's truth fearlessly, without any unbiblical qualifications, without dulling the edge of the divine sword, and without omitting anything that might be "profitable"[3] in the lives of counselees. That requires a bold,[4] straightforward presentation of truth.

Listen once more to those words in II Timothy 2:15: "cutting the Word of truth with accuracy" (literally, "cutting it straight"). The idea here seems to be that of a workman such as a carpenter or stone mason cutting wood or stone *exactly* so that it fits the space for which it is intended. If one cuts a board to fit in one place, but tries to use it elsewhere where it doesn't fit, he will botch the job. Each board must be measured and cut to fit into the place in which it belongs – then placed *there*.[5] Accurate

---

1 Let God do it for you instead of you.
2 Against the biblical use of the law for life.
3 Or "beneficial;" cf. Acts 20:20.
4 The Greek word is *parresia*, meaning "truth spoken without fear of consequences."
5 In his commentary on II Timothy, Calvin spoke of cutting pieces from a loaf suitable to each individual member of a family.

cutting of God's Word, then, has to do not only with the proper selection of materials, but also with specific application – fitting God's truth into lives of particular persons in specific situations. **Effective implementation** is the fourth and final step. Many are good at explaining the "what to" of a passage, but are quite defective when it comes to suggesting any "how to." Yet right here is where counselees frequently fail. They may *want* to do as instructed, *attempt* to do it, but fall flat on their faces because of flawed implementation of a biblical command. They don't know how to "get it in gear." Jesus' Sermon on the Mount (Matthew 5–7) teaches us the importance of helping people to implement truth. After the beatitudes and the general comments on salt and light, Jesus showed his listeners *how to* implement all of the subsequent commands that He gave them so as to be able to carry them out.[1]

Your counselees will come alive and then grow rapidly when you show them how to implement biblical truth. But they cannot continue to depend on you to do this for them. That's why it may be very important, as soon after the turning point as possible, to introduce them to a Bible study course such as *What to do on Thursday*. Here they will find instruction in implementation as well as in selection, interpretation, and application. Above all, this practical Bible study method is adaptable to laymen.

All four of the elements in CARE are important for the counselor but they are important for counselees as well. To keep them from having to return again for more help in the future, you need to help them learn how to receive and follow *God's* counsel directly from His Word. You have not served your counselees well if you fail to do this along with everything else. You must do everything possible to avoid making counselees dependent on you.

---

1 For details, see my book *Preaching with Purpose.*

Chapter Thirteen

Don't Choke
Your Counselee

In this trilogy I have been covering much material; perhaps you would say *too* much. You may protest, "How do you expect me to remember everything? It just seems too difficult." I beg to differ. If you are one who has been called by God to ministry, by His wisdom and grace, you can learn, you can improve, you can show progress that will be evident to all. I have tried to cover only essentials; there is much more that I could have written, and in other books, you will find some of it there. And I have tried to present what you have in your hands as succinctly and straightforwardly as possible.

Remember, in these three books I am *analyzing* counseling procedures. "Analysis," by its nature, takes things apart in order to look at each piece of the whole. You do not drive a car in pieces (unless yours looks like mine!); you drive a car that is a whole – it has an exhaust system, a fuel system, an electrical system, and the like, all coordinated with the chassis and the body so that the entire automobile moves as a whole, each part functioning together with the others. These counseling elements also work together in the one person who practices them. What I have been teaching here comes together in the counselor *as he counsels.*[1]

---

1 Counselees (and counselors in training) who have observed veteran biblical counselors at work will testify that they do everything almost automatically. But you may be sure what is now "second nature" for them was not so at first. Like you, they had to learn the elements before they could put them together. Indeed, experienced counselors may find that this analysis of the three most crucial periods in counseling will help them check up on their practices and will serve as a refresher. Once you have learned how to counsel, it is easy to go to the opposite extreme and become overconfident or even complacent. Those who do this may discover that they are omitting important elements from their counseling.

Christian counselors have been doing what is outlined here for over 30 years. If you should ask them how they learned to do so, I am confident that they would tell you that it seemed complicated at first, but that after they learned gradually, what they do now comes habitually. It is usually only at first, while learning, that difficulties in remembering arise. But after a time everything becomes easier and easier to remember until there is no difficulty at all. One way to keep abreast is to prayerfully read the sections of these books that you have the most difficulty remembering, prior to each day of counseling. In time, you too will find everything coming together.

But of equal importance is trying not to do too much with your counselee in the period following the turning point. If you can recognize the difficulties that you may be having learning new things, remember, he will be facing similar difficulties too. And he may not have as much time as you do. Your counselee needs time to assimilate and consolidate the gains that he has made. He will, therefore, do best by focusing on the new ways and thoughts that he is learning with reference to his fundamental problems. If you attempt to solve all other ancillary problems that may arise during counseling, not only will you extend counseling too far and tend to encourage the counselee to become dependent on you, but you may also choke him by putting too much on his plate at one time. It is better to solve the critical issues, demonstrate clearly how the issues were solved, and set in place new attitudes and practices that he may use over and over to solve other problems later on his own.

For instance, if a husband and his wife learn how to use the conference table effectively (see page 67) they should be able to solve all sorts of problems that they had no way of solving before. Moreover, one reason I have suggested that you start your counselee on the course of practical Bible study that is found in *What to Do on Thursday* is so that he will have a methodology for using the Scriptures to deal with matters that arise during the week.

I have compared your own learning with that of your counselee and urged you not to choke him with too much change all at once. Perhaps in that way you can best see what I have in mind in this chapter. But there are ways in which the comparison fails. You are a counselor – or would be one. He is a counselee. Presumably, though there is much to learn, your own spiritual life is moving in the right direction. The counselee has been going astray. He is weak and still has many ragged edges that need filing; presumably, you have already been doing that for some time. The counselee may still be reeling from some of his assignments, which may have been very difficult for him to accomplish. He may be spiritually exhausted. Pile another of these on him at this time and he may collapse!

On the other hand, the good that has been done must be sustained. I have warned about the tendency for the counselee to think that everything has been done that needs to be done by making the breakthrough. Make it clear that this only affords the possibility for more progress; it is but a new beginning. It provides the opportunity to deal with many other issues that have arisen, and also to uncover and deal with others. But they can not all be done at once.

So what you want to do is to concentrate on establishing firmly what you have achieved so that there is no reversion to the past. That is one reason why I have stressed changes of associates, putting on new ways to replace old ones, etc. These are all important to rooting and grounding the counselee. But they take time. The key thing in this period, then, is consolidation (further consolidation will be needed at termination as well). That is the principal effort to be made. Be sure, therefore, you do not refocus your counselee's attention on new material that will divert him from doing the work he must do in firmly establishing the new ways. While it is always important for you to hold out the need for continued progress, make it clear that he isn't ready to attack too much more at once. My warning here is simply this: don't let him push you into letting him bite off more than he can chew. You will need wisdom to determine how much he can take on. Some will have more enthusiasm than knowledge or ability. Others may be able to do more at a faster rate. But all along, you ought to be assessing this matter so that when the counselee has turned the corner, you will be able to determine how far and how fast you can go with him at that point and how much you should hold him back from plunging forward too quickly.

It is not that I am encouraging you to keep a counselee from progressing to new and greater heights in his Christian life; it is that he will not build for the future unless he builds on a solid foundation. You must be sure that during this period you do all you can to lay the foundation for the future well. That is the point!

When we move to the third book in this trilogy, which has to do with concluding formal counseling, you will see once again that I will warn about the matter of moving too rapidly. But you will also see that I will anticipate greater progress after the conclusion of formal counseling. There I will encourage the counselee to take on new projects *on his own*. And I hope to help you to prepare him to do just that before you dismiss him from counseling. I will also suggest ways of following up this progress so that if it goes wrong you may not only correct it, but will also be able to use that failure to further instruct the counselee. But that is for the next book in the series; I mention it here just to let you know that this is not the end. But it is important to view the post-breakthrough period as a time to pause, to take a breath, to take stock of where you are, and to consolidate the gains made thus far. If you can achieve that, you will have done much – more, perhaps, than either you or your counselee realizes. The key here is to so reorient the counselee that he neither wants to nor is able to revert to his old ways. That is your fundamental task in this time.

How long will the post-breakthrough period last before termination of counseling? I will discuss this point more fully in the next book, but for now, let me say that you must prolong it as long as it takes to solidify the new lifestyle, but no longer. Again, be careful not to let the counselee build a dependence upon you. The way in which you do the first and at the same time avoid the latter is to set up some situations (realistic ones, that have to do with the milieu in which he lives) that will give you and the counselee opportunities to assert his new understandings and commitments. How well he achieves this will be your index for determining how much longer the post-breakthrough period should continue. You want to reach termination as quickly as possible, but not so quickly that the counselee has had no opportunity to put the new ways into practice and to regularly come out on the positive side. Ordinarily – and notice this qualification – for most experienced counselors this period will last four to six weeks.[1] Some counselees will require longer periods of work and testing; most will not. You must determine – wisely.

So, let me say it again: this is a period in which wisdom on the part of the counselor predominates. There are no direct Scripture verses that may be applied to amounts of time and the rate of progress one may make during the period we are discussing. Nevertheless, the principles of gradual progress imbedded in the word *prokope* ("progress") mentioned before, and Hebrews' idea that people are not always ready for something until something else in their lives happens first (Hebrews 5:11) lie behind all that I have been trying to say. Be sure that you take this discussion to heart, or you may find the work that you have done collapsing before you since the foundation is weak. Firmly establish the counselee before moving on!

---

1 An inexperienced counselor may take a bit longer. But he should never let his early cases set the standard for later ones. As he improves, he will discover that doing the same things, and achieving the same results, will take him less time. The important thing here is to be certain that the same results are accomplished.

Conclusion

I urge you to think about the matters in each book in this trilogy in relationship to the other two. The three books are distinct in order to emphasize the distinct nature of each phase of formal counseling but all three sections are necessary to understanding the process as a whole.

It is possible, of course, to lose a counselee at any point in counseling,[1] but that is most likely to happen at one of the three crucial points – especially at the first two. Therefore, I urge you to devour the items in these books, put them into practice, and continue to follow them as you learn to counsel more effectively.

There are other books that will help you in the process of counseling, some of which have information that also fits into the orb of the three crucial points discussed here that I have omitted rather than repeat my other books. I refer especially to *The Christian Counselor's Manual* and to the specialty volumes: *The Handbook of Church Discipline, How to Help People Change, The Theology of Counseling, From Forgiven to Forgiving, Solving Marriage Problems,* and *Marriage, Divorce and Remarriage in the Bible.* You may wish to thumb through these at your local Christian bookstore and determine which, if any, might aid you in counseling.

---

1 Unexpected changes in their situations occur, people refuse to do homework, and many other matters may occasion the loss. But when one or more of the three crucial points emphasized by this trilogy is poorly executed, they are more likely to cease counseling. That is one reason you should be certain that you understand and do those things that facilitate proper movement from the first session through termination.

CRITICAL STAGES
of BIBLICAL
COUNSELING

Finishing Well
The Termination *of* Biblical Counseling

Jay E. Adams

Finishing Well
The Termination
of Biblical Counseling

Contents

Introduction

The two previous books in this trilogy dealt with the first session and the session in which there was a breakthrough in counseling. This book concerns all those basic issues that have to do with closing out a series of counseling sessions – how you know when to do so, how you do it, how you can make certain that you have done the right thing, how you may follow up. It also deals with those not-so-happy experiences in which there is an abrupt termination at a disadvantageous time, when the termination is ragged, and when the termination turns out to be precipitous or immature. The discussion will also include a summary of the entire trilogy.

I hope not only that this trilogy will give the new would-be counselor valuable insights and information of a sort that is focused on the three critical sessions singled out, but that it will be a useful refresher for those who have been counseling for some time. It is all too easy to forget things when one becomes used to a routine. Sometimes important issues are omitted, not remembered, or by-passed in the effort to get things done. For such experienced counselors, this trilogy should prove valuable in reminding them of matters once known but long since forgotten, in helping them to evaluate current practices, and even in introducing them to new ways in which to sharpen their current attitudes, biblical understandings, and methodologies. In short, I have tried to deal with issues with which any counselor should become familiar, whether he is new to the work or seasoned in it. It is my desire to see these goals fulfilled.

As you probably can see at the outset, the material covered in the three books is preeminently practical. It does deal with more than mechanics, however. I have mentioned attitudes. I want you to know that I consider attitude very important. Moreover, I have discussed atmosphere. Nothing could be more important than to bring counselees into direct relationship with God. I have discussed these two matters in *Getting Started*. But even though I have not reemphasized them in the second and third books, what is found in either of the previous books is *assumed* in later ones.

When I mentioned writing the trilogy to a friend and trusted counselor, he particularly liked the idea of discussing the termination of counseling. He commented that this is an area that needs elucidation, and he pointed out how difficult it often is to know how long to continue and when to terminate, and to have a way of determining whether the decision was good or bad. Moreover, he said, it would be valuable to have a way of recouping if it becomes clear that the decision was flawed.

Those matters are clearly in view as I write. I hope to give satisfying, biblically-based answers to all of these matters. My desire is to help all who read this trilogy to become more effective counselors to the honor of God and the blessing of His people.

Chapter One

Everything Must End

Both the counselor and the counselee look forward to an end of counseling. They know that it can't go on forever! Seeing the end is one thing that keeps them going, as Paul says in I Corinthians 10:13: "a way out, that you may be able to endure it." But there are many questions that must be answered before terminating counseling. I have mentioned some of them in the introduction. Here, I simply want to stress that since there will be an end, it is important to plan for it, so that it will come at the right time, in the right way, for the right reasons. It is easy for a counselee or a counselor to bring counseling to an end wrongly. That is what must be avoided if at all possible.

Do you *plan* for the termination of counseling? Or do you simply let it come about in whatever way it might? Many counselors do the latter rather than the former. Of course, there are enough contingencies in counseling that it is not possible to plan exactly how or when a given counseling case may end, but there are certainly enough commonalties in all cases that there is much that may be planned and followed. And no matter how different the particulars of a counseling case may be, each case has goals to shoot for. That is what I mean by planning.

Counseling, in most instances, should neither end abruptly nor simply peter out. There should be some indication to the counselee that things are drawing to a close, so that like the passenger who fastens his seat belt, the counselee knows that the plane is about to land.

One way in which a counselor may indicate that counseling is about to close is to inform the counselee at the outset that "*ordinarily*,[1] counseling will last a maximum of twelve weeks." This not only gives him some idea from the start about what he

---

1 Be sure you qualify this statement in this way. New counselors may take longer to achieve the same results that seasoned counselors do. Keep that in

is committing himself to, but around the tenth session or so, I have had counselees comment on the fact that they have only two more weeks to go; believe me, they count the weeks. But be sure to emphasize the word "ordinarily," since you may find it necessary to terminate counseling later on. Often, when one knows that the end is drawing near, he begins to apply himself all the more assiduously to what he has to do. Timing, then, is one important factor in planning the termination of counseling.

Noting that the end is in view may also provide help in warning lax counselees, encouraging reluctant ones, and refreshing weary ones. In other words, it gives everyone something to shoot at. But, as I indicated, you should not allow a counselee to think that counseling has been extended because he has failed, when he has not. Sometimes you may have to tell a counselee that the reason counseling must be extended is that his case is unusual, other unexpected factors have arisen, or something of the sort. On the other hand, when the counselee's failure to do his homework is the cause for extending counseling, make it clear that is the case. Indeed, at times you may set a second goal for terminating counseling that must be reached at all costs, because you will not be willing to go on longer beyond it – though be sure of yourself before doing so. Sometimes, that will speed up action by the counselee in a remarkable way.

So termination itself may become a powerful, effective tool in counseling. It must be viewed not simply as something that happens, but as something that you *use* for purposes that, unless you recognize them, you may neglect. You, or your counselee, *cause* it to happen.

Is there biblical precedent for the use of time in influencing others? In II Corinthians 13:2, Paul, speaking of "those who sinned before while I was present with you," wrote, "I say it in

---

mind whenever you suggest general lengths of time to a counselee. To lay out some amount of time as a goal helps counselees know that counseling will not be interminable as, for instance, psychotherapy is. Moreover, setting time goals gives a counselee hope. He sees that you actually anticipate that God will make a genuine change in his situation.

advance...that when I come to you again I won't spare them." He was sending signals ahead about what he would do – and when. Then, later on in the chapter, he wrote, "I am writing these things to you while I am absent, so that when I am present I won't have to cut off any of you by the authority that the Lord gave me for building up and not for tearing down" (v. 10).

While his situation was not precisely parallel to yours, you can see how well he used time and future goals in warning in order to bring about change in the lives of some who were not doing what God wanted them to do. Notice also I Corinthians 16:1–8; II Corinthians 2:1–3; 10:11; 12:14, 20–21 for additional examples of how Paul set forth time-frames that were designed to urge his readers to solve problems that they had delayed dealing with.

At any rate, it is crucial to recognize time as a valuable tool in counseling[1] – especially the time frame that leads to the termination of counseling. When you do so, you will find that hints of termination may be one of your most powerful tools for helping slothful or reluctant counselees to speed up the process of counseling.

A misconception about termination that I want to clear up in this book is that termination means washing your hands of a counselee. I shall have to spend time discussing the ways in which termination is brought about so that a transition is made that will provide for follow-up and continued improvement. Counseling is but a segment in the sanctification of a counselee,

---

1 Other time factors may also be used as a tool. For instance, you may refuse to "waste time" in conducting a counseling session when a counselee comes to counseling with his homework not accomplished. You may say to him, "We simply cannot go on until this work is done; what follows is dependent on its accomplishment. So we have lost this session." You may then send the counselee home to complete his work, or into another room to do so. But you have said that you cannot go on, so don't. This sort of use of time is very valuable in emphasizing that you are serious about homework assignments and that you believe in the proper, productive use of time. You are not going to spend the session simply wasting time in chit-chat; sessions must be going somewhere, or they should not be conducted at all.

in which he is helped to overcome some difficulty from which he is unable to extricate himself on his own (Galatians 6:1ff.). By the way that they act, some counselors give the appearance that they think that counseling is everything. Though counseling may be of great importance, it is but a blip on the radar scene of your counselee's life. When a counselor views counseling in its proper perspective, it will make a great difference in how he conducts counseling and, in particular, how he terminates it. As a counselor, you will consider yourself obligated at termination to do all that you can to commend your counselee to God and to His Word of grace as it is ministered in a true church of the Lord Jesus Christ (cf. Acts 20:32). When you reflect upon the fact that what you do in counseling will be terminated, you will begin to take a more humble attitude toward yourself and your work as a counselor. In a sense you are a repair man who comes in to fix the leaky faucet. You are the agency to which the counselee brings his automobile for service that he cannot give it himself. But while the matters with which you deal are, I admit, vastly more important, your place is as limited as the plumber's or the automobile mechanic's. Let the brevity of counseling teach you not to think more highly of yourself than you ought to.

Termination, then, is a healthy thing for both the counselor and the counselee. Freud said that, ideally, counseling should never end. And given the parameters of what he believed, he was correct. He thought that a person had to be resocialized. But first, in analyzing previous, wrong socialization, that would mean going back through the rivers that constitute the ocean that the counselee now is, to the streams that make up the rivers, and to the creeks that flow into the rivers, and ultimately to the springs of his past. By the time one could do so (even if it were possible), the counselee would have become a new and different ocean. But you shouldn't have such an exalted view of your counseling. You must see your task ordinarily as little more than repairing something that has broken down.[1] You help fix it, by

---

1 Of course, I am not talking here about educational counseling such as pre-

God's grace, from His Word, send the counselee back to all of the various discipling activities in his church, and go on to the next case.[1]

---

marital counseling, vocational counseling, and the like. In such counseling, the work is preliminary, precautionary, and preventive.

1 I shall add to this later on. The matter of follow-up cannot be discussed here.

Chapter Two

What is Termination?

"Everyone knows what termination means, doesn't he?" Well, we shall see. If by the word you mean simply ending counseling, then you have too narrow an understanding of the term. Termination involves the termination of sin, wrong ways, faulty thinking and attitudes, as well as the termination of counseling sessions. While these two sides to termination will never coincide perfectly in this life, there should be correspondence between the solutions to problems presented in counseling and the termination of counseling sessions, such that the two coincide. Ideally, you should end counseling because you have eliminated the problem that required counseling in the first place. Though the ideal and the actual rarely correspond exactly, to bring them together as closely as possible ought to be the counselor's goal. So termination is not so simple as it might seem at first. Termination means termination of the *need* for counseling, which leads to the termination of counseling sessions themselves.

In this book, I not only shall attempt to help you to assess whether or not the time for termination has come, but shall mention several ways to reach the goal of proper termination. Unless there is a denouement satisfying to both the counselor and the counselee, termination probably should not occur. If the counselor is satisfied, but the counselee is not, that may be due to a misunderstanding. It may be because the counselee wanted more than he could have or more than the counselor was able or willing to impart. If the counselor is dissatisfied, but counselee is satisfied, that situation may arise from error on the part of the counselor, but most likely from the unwillingness of a counselor to settle for as little as the counselee. He sees more that may be done, sees the need to consolidate gains, or something of the sort. So there are several angles from which to view the act of bringing the counseling to an end.

Then there is another factor to consider. Counseling must not, as I intimated in the last chapter, be the end of growth, change, discipleship, and the like on the part of the counselee. What happens after counseling depends on the relationships among the counselor, the counselee, and the church. The counselee may experience a very natural transition back into the normal, ongoing nurture of his congregation, with no need for more than regular pastoral care. If this is not a possibility for the counselee, counseling may result in a number of other changes that lead toward strengthening, rooting, and grounding the counselee in his new ways (see page 89ff.). These changes may even involve, in extreme cases, the transition of the counselee to a different, more biblical congregation that will carry on nurturing care and discipline. So termination may also involve abrupt, unnatural changes as well as smooth, natural ones. Termination, then, must not be thought of only in terms of what now ceases; it must also be viewed in the light of what must follow it. Few insights into termination could be more important, and I shall treat this matter in some depth in this book.

"Well," you say, "I never thought about termination in that way before." If that is true of you as a novice counselor, or a somewhat seasoned counselor, then unless you do begin to view and treat termination in this manner, you will find that much of your counseling will be undone in the days or months that follow termination. This is disheartening to your counselee and ought to be so to you as well. Of course, proper termination can never assure that everything will go well – there are so many things that might go wrong, many of which neither you nor your counselee can foresee – but, surely, as a good, biblical counselor, you must do all that you can to guard against the sorts of evils that might arise. In this book, I shall attempt to help in this matter as well.

Finally, termination is not, as you can see, "cutting someone loose." It is not merely a matter of leaving something, but is a transition *to* something. Unless that is true, the vacuum problem mentioned in *Breaking Through* (page 146) is likely to take over; if the counselee is not moved into the right thing, he is likely to drift into the wrong one. Biblical counselors must take responsibility for what happens to the counselee when he leaves counseling, while taking care not to create dependency upon themselves.

You realize, I hope, from this brief survey of what is involved in termination, that there is much to consider about the matter. Don't think that it is unimportant or that there is only one way to deal with the matter. There is much to learn. Chances are, you have not given adequate thought to this issue. I hope that this book will challenge you and help you to do so.

Chapter Three

Terminating Problems

The termination of counseling sessions is not dependent solely upon the number of sessions conducted, nor the estimate of time allotted, though these factors have a bearing upon it. It is principally determined by solving the problem or problems that were the focus of the counseling.

Now, that does not mean that every problem uncovered in counseling sessions must be solved before terminating sessions. Quite to the contrary. After the counselee makes a breakthrough concerning his main difficulties, a wise counselor will instruct as he goes along, demonstrating how to deal with life's difficulties. This will prepare the counselee to solve many of the less-involved problems that arose during counseling, even after the counseling process has ended. The biblical counselor wants the counselee to be able to deal with problems on his own rather than having to return to counseling for every future difficulty he encounters.

In a sense, you might say that the biblical counselor is looking for at least *two* turning points in counseling. The first we discussed in book two of this trilogy, *Breaking Through: The Turning Point of Biblical Counseling*. This is the breakthrough in the presentation problem. But, in addition, I suggest that good counselors don't settle for that alone. If there is any way to do so, they work just as hard to teach and train counselees how to solve problems on their own. They use the very problem on which they have been working as a teaching model for handling matters that will yet transpire in the life of the counselee.

Sometimes the example will have to be a negative one, at least to an extent – if the counselee was reluctant to do what God commands, if he stumbled and reverted to past ways, if he misunderstood and temporarily went off on the wrong path. But the counselor will use even these sins as teaching examples not only of what not to do, but also of how to recoup from failure through repentance and change.

Moreover, the counselor will often also institute certain practices during counseling that help to solve the problems that they are dealing with. These practices (such as the conference table, see page 67ff.) may be generalized to other life problems as well. So, having learned to use them efficiently, the counselee may be urged to continue them long after counseling sessions have ceased.[1] In these ways, the counselor attempts to do two things at once. As he is introducing solutions and practices, the counselor may not trouble the counselee with the idea that he is teaching for the long haul. That may seem too much for the counselee at the time (cf. John 16:12).[2] But after successfully working to achieve those goals that the Bible sets forth, the counselee will be more amenable to learning them and using them as a part of his sanctification repertoire, as were the disciples after the resurrection.

Termination of certain problems in counseling, then, will be a large factor in determining when the termination of counseling sessions should take place. Another factor will be the rooting and grounding of the counselee in loving obedience to the will of God (Ephesians 3:17). If one is still very weak, extending counseling a session or two may be exactly what is needed. The key here is that, since the breakthrough, the counselee has faced some temptation and has stood fast, thereby demonstrating that the new ways have begun to take root in him and he in them. He must not be turned loose if he is likely to be blown about by every wind of doctrine, for instance. More time should be expended to assure that he is firmly planted in the truth. Nor should he be dismissed from counseling if he is apt to fall in the face of some temptation. Again, in such cases, time should be

---

1 There are many useful practices of this sort. For some examples (list-making, using the DPP form, etc.), see *The Christian Counselor's Manual*.

2 It is wrong to dump too much on counselees all at once. Jesus recognized His disciple's capacities for receiving and learning and gave them what they needed *when they were able to bear it* – not before. You must do the same.

extended. Rooting and grounding the counselee is, therefore, vital to determining when to terminate sessions.

There are persons who have a low view of sanctification. Of course, it is impossible for one to become perfectly sanctified in this life. But some seem to think that there is very little progress that anyone can make. By what they write, it seems that they think that a person is never able to put a sinful way of life behind him. Not only does that demean the grace of God, but it is a totally unbiblical concept. They teach something like an AA view of the Christian life: there is no significant progress, and every morning as he looks himself in the mirror, one must reiterate, for instance, "I am still an adulterer who must take it one day at a time, attempting not to commit adultery today."

Now, that low view of the grace of God in sanctification is countered by the Scriptures, which after listing almost every life-dominating sin in the book (I Corinthians 6:9–10) go on to say, "And these are what some of you *were...*" (I Corinthians 6:11). Notice the past tense. Those words indicate something better than an AA view of sanctification! Here were people who, by God's grace, were "washed and *sanctified*" (v. 11) as well as "justified." Was the apostle Paul, who had been a murderer prior to his conversion (Acts 9:1), unable to put that in the past? Or, as these dismal interpreters think, was he forced to face the temptation to murder others every remaining day of his life? The idea is preposterous as well as unbiblical.

So while always remembering a weak counselee may fall back into former sinful ways, that is not inevitable. And one thing that will forestall such a sad event is taking the time to be sure that there has been proper rooting and grounding in love. Love is a powerful force, much more powerful than temptation. Keep that in mind and be sure that the changes that your counselee manifests are direct, as well as indirect, fulfillments of the two great commandments to love God and neighbor. That is the principal way to avoid failure.

If a counselee does fall, that is not an indication that counseling has been worthless. Jesus didn't give up on the stumbling Peter, who denied Him three times, nor did he give up on the

Corinthian church with all its problems. Rather, through repentance He restored him as many times as he had fallen (John 21), and He also recommissioned him for future ministry as well. Don't despair if such a thing takes place; and don't let your fallen counselee despair either. Remind him of the story of Peter's fall and restoration. But be sure to do so in such a way that he understands that Peter was held fully responsible for his sin, as he too will be.

Termination of counseling sessions, then, is only one sort of termination toward which the biblical counselor works. Keep that in mind; it is easy to forget.

Chapter Four
Termination as Transition

Biblical counseling is part of the special care and discipline of Christ's church, and often involves both. When a counselee is dismissed from counseling, however, he is not dismissed from the church's care and discipline. Instead, he transitions into the general care and discipline of the church. This general care involves the regular ministry of the Word as it is preached from week to week, the discipling process carried on by groups or individuals, the love and good works of believers one toward another, pastoral care, and the like. So right thinking about the matter of termination will always sees it as a process of *transition* back into the fullness of the general care and discipline of the congregation to which one belongs – or to which he is transferring.

It would be wrong, however, in saying this to think of the period one is in counseling as a time when he no longer is under the church's general care. Indeed, if that care is lax or he withdraws himself from it, the biblical counselor will do all that he can to bring him back under that care. He knows that it is not right to forsake the assembling together of believers (Hebrews 10:25), and knows that all that he is doing in counseling is only supplementary to and must be buttressed by the general ministry of the church. It is against the background of that ministry, then, that he counsels.

Sadly, there are times when the general ministry of the Word is weaker than the specific ministry of counseling. In such cases, the counselor (presuming he is someone other than the pastor of the church that the counselee is a member of) must himself provide a modicum of the general nurture and direction that ought to back up what he is doing.[1] In extreme cases, the

---

1 The counselor cannot do it all. When it is necessary for him to do this, he must be particularly careful not to cultivate dependence on counseling. It is

181

situation may be so bad (e.g., the church refuses to discipline virtually declaring itself a non-church) that the counselor must advise changing congregations. This can be precarious for all concerned. Nevertheless, if the counselee's congregation refuses to do as it ought, and refuses offers from the counselor to assist, the counselor has no choice but to advise changing congregations.[1] This is a very sad situation and calls for careful evaluation and caution. Nevertheless, today there are many congregations purporting to be biblical that refuse to function according to the Scriptures. When there is steadfast refusal to follow Scripture, under those circumstances, there may be no other choice.

When termination is viewed as transition – as it should be – that makes a very great difference in how the counselor thinks about dismissing his counselee from counseling and, therefore, how he does so. He doesn't say "good-bye" and then virtually wash his hands of the counselee. Rather, he will make decided efforts to see to it that the proper transition is made smoothly. If he is the pastor, or an elder of the counselee's congregation, the transition may be quite natural. Under those circumstances, the counselor will provide whatever discipleship is necessary, calling on one or more of his members to become disciplers of the former counselee, he will urge attendance of all the regular services and suggest other programs or meetings that would strengthen the counselee.[2] In other words, if the transition is "in house," as it should be, the opportunity for a smooth transition is naturally present – and if the counselor is aware of the need for it, he should have little trouble effecting it.

However, there are many cases where the counselee is from another congregation than the counselor (see also page 111ff.

---

those circumstances especially that breed dependency if he is not aware of the fact and does not guard against it. Though a counselee may try to find in counseling what he cannot find in his congregation, counseling cannot provide that for him because of the basic limitations of its nature and purposes.

1 For details on declaring a congregation a non-church, and relating to it and its members as such, see my book, *The Handbook of Church Discipline*.

2 Such as special courses in Bible interpretation, family life, etc.

and page 140ff.). In such instances the counselor will have required either the pastor or an elder of the counselee's church to be present during counseling sessions. Their presence not only demonstrates concern for their member in this way, and enables them to have a knowledge of what has been happening in his life, but ideally, they also provide the link with the counselee's congregation by which the termination transition may take place.

Often, when such a transition is made to the counselee's congregation through an elder or pastor, the counselor will "hand off" the counselee earlier than he would were he himself to counsel through to completion. When this happens, it is necessary for all concerned to know what is happening. Doing this enables the counselor to open the hour to other counselees, enables the counselee's church to minister to him once the counseling has gotten over the hump, and allows the counselee to see that his own church cares for him.

When a counselee is handed over to his own pastor and elders before the completion of counseling, this should be done with full instructions about where to go from here. Not only should the counselee be given a set of homework assignments for the ensuing weeks, but the pastor of his church (who has now become counselor) should be instructed about where to go next. Indeed, the former counselor probably ought to have a strategy conference with the counselee's pastor about such matters and, having dismissed the counselee into the special care of his church, the counselor should offer to be available to the counselee's pastor for future consultation either over the phone or in person. In the unlikely case where things go very wrong after dismissal into the pastor's care, the counselor may even suggest that they return for a session or two.

It is critical for a counselor to know *when* is the best time to make the transition to the counselee's own pastor. Usually, this will be during the rooting and grounding period following the turning point in which gains made thus far are being consolidated. That is usually the sort of thing – given proper instruction – that most faithful pastors can do well.

Transitions are not always smooth. Sometimes a counselee will declare that he is not ready to leave counseling. I have mentioned this before. Under such circumstances, the counselor must probe (often deeply) to discover what is behind that objection. Many possibilities may arise. The counselee may be developing an unhealthy dependency. Termination could not be more important in such cases. In other instances, there may be some matter that the counselee wants to resolve before counseling has been completed. If this is a secondary matter that you think he would be wise tackling on his own (as I have suggested in a previous chapter), explain why you want him to do so and that you are convinced of his ability under God to do it. You might even mention, and exposit, Philippians 2:12–13, where Paul makes it clear that, though he couldn't be present to work out the solution to the problem of disunity in the congregation, God would be with the church enabling them to have the right desires and ability to do so without him.[1]

On the other hand, there may be important matters that counselees have kept back, hidden until the time when you are about to terminate counseling. Why they do so may differ in each case. Perhaps the counselee wanted to test you with other matters first, just to see how good you were, what sorts of things you would require, whether he thought you could handle lesser problems. Perhaps he has been embarrassed to bring it up, reluctant to divulge some scarlet sin. After you have successfully helped him to meet other matters, and after seeing that you are not an ogre with three eyes in the middle of your head, he is at last willing to bring the matter to the surface. It may be that he sees this as a last resort. In such cases, you may have another

---

1 This passage is not talking about eternal salvation, or working out the implications thereof. The Philippians were already saved. "Salvation" here means going through a difficult situation successfully (see a similar use of the word "salvation" in Philippians 1:19, KJV). That they were to solve the problem of disunity *on their own*, apart from Paul's presence, is the point of referring to this passage (see also 1:17). Philippians 2:13 makes it abundantly clear that we are never really on our own; God is there urging us on and helping us to do His will whenever we are willing to do it. Stress this fact.

counseling case on your hands, not from a different counselee, but from the same one.

At this point, you have some decisions to make. Will you continue? Will you hand this case over to another counselor, or will you continue to deal with him yourself? The latter would be the ideal. You have built a relationship of trust and understanding; he knows you and how you work, you know him and how he functions. But sometimes the fresh approach of another counselor (his pastor or one of your elders) is precisely what is needed; he might be taking you for granted, he may be developing dependency. You may have allotted the time for another counselee who desperately needs help, and cannot afford to give him the time the newly surfaced problem may require. If you decide not to continue, be sure to let him know the reason.

Moreover, take this opportunity to explain to him how important it is to let a counselor know about such problems early on so that he can plan his time well. Part of what you are always concerned to help a counselee do is to become more considerate of others and their time. Many counselees are very inconsiderate in this way and need to be taught that there are other people in the world with problems besides themselves.

The important thing, then, is to see that a transition is made. You cannot always achieve this. There are times when people move or get upset and end counseling themselves, have tragic events occur in their lives that upset counseling, and the like; all of which which disrupt smooth transitions that you are attempting to make. In such cases, you may simply commend them to God. What you cannot do by His grace, He can do without you – quite well, if you please! But always think "transition" when you think termination. That is the point of this chapter.

Chapter Five

Attitudes

There is an important matter that is seldom mentioned in regard to termination – the attitudes with which a counselee leaves counseling. Termination ought to be not so much a time of apprehension, which may come from too great a dependency on the counselor, as a time of anticipation. It is this spirit of hope and expectancy that you will want to cultivate through the exposition of biblical passages that inculcate it. Now that the presentation problems are resolved, the weight of their pressure is lifted and vistas for service stretch before him unimpeded by difficulties as had been the case in the past. The counselee ought to go forth from counseling determined to do what he could not do before.

Moreover, he now ought to see certain areas of need in his life, which he should be ready to meet in various ways. Perhaps he has been a weak Bible student, and counseling has brought him to the place where he now can see the need to learn his Bible better. Possibly he has been a poor parent who knows that he must get such things in order for the future. It may be that he understands his place in relationship to God and his neighbor in a much clearer way now and is anxious to cement the right kind of ties from now on. He may have learned to replace sinful old ways with righteous new ones in one or two areas, but having once understood the put off/put on dynamic,[1] he is now desirous of extending this to other areas of his life. In other words, his attitude should be one of hopeful expectancy for the days to come.

Now, this expectancy ought not to be merely some vague, undefined anticipation of hope. No, it ought to center on specific items. The counselor will probably want to help him focus on these. He may do so by assigning homework in which the

---

1 For details on this dynamic, see *The Christian Counselor's Manual.*

counselee makes an initial inventory of his life and lists at least two items in each of several areas of his life where growth in Christian living and service is needed. Prior to termination he will bring these to counseling and the counselor will help him to go over them, placing them in some order of priority for the counselee since it is likely that he cannot change on all fronts at once. Perhaps this list ought to be brought into counseling at the session before the next to last session. In that way there is ample time to help the counselee get started before termination. The counselor can see enough of the work done to determine whether the counselee is headed in the right direction, and perhaps to make certain vital corrections with reference thereto. The counselee leaves on a high point of activity; termination does not mean the cessation of activity. The counselee's attitude ought to be, "Now I can really 'get at' the business of improving some of the other areas of my life."

In his exuberance over having overcome a long-standing or particularly burdensome problem, he may want to take on too much at once. Help him to moderate his enthusiasm by making reasonable long-term goals. He may want to bite off more than he is able to chew, which is likely to result in failure. That can be quite discouraging for a counselee whose expectations are riding high. Your task, then, is to help him adopt a *realistic* attitude about the future.

On the other hand, there is the fearful counselee who, being "cut loose" from counseling, anticipates nothing but future failure. He must be encouraged by the use of Scripture to look forward to the future with hope and anticipation of growth and greater confidence. After all, he has been able to overcome a large problem; why should he think that in the future things will be different? The same Lord, using the same Word, will bring about the same results – assuming he trusts and follows His Word. He must be assured that it was God Who made the difference, and not the counselor or he himself. It is God upon Whom he can depend in the days to come. Make it clear that if he depends on anything or anyone else, he will fail; but there is no reason to expect this if he is trusting in the Lord to help him.

Hold forth the prospect of growth and strength. Use passages such as Ephesians 1:15–21, I Corinthians 10:13, Romans 15:4, 13 to foster such hope and expectation.[1]

In other words, every counselee ought to leave counseling not merely with a sense of relief ("at last the problem is solved").

Rather, in gratitude, he ought to view termination as an opportunity to make great strides in his Christian faith, an opportunity to enter into service for the Lord as never before, and an opportunity to help others who may also be struggling with problems that they cannot resolve on their own (Galatians 6:1ff.). This spirit of gratitude to God is important.

With reference to helping others with their problems, you may need to warn the counselee not to brag about what has happened to him (remind him of I Corinthians 10:12). Encourage him to wait until he is spiritually strong enough and wise enough to help; though he should not wait too long, using lack of readiness as an excuse for inactivity. Help him ascertain what kind of help he is or isn't able to offer at any given time. There are some who, having gone through counseling successfully, think that this qualifies them to be counselors. Remind them of Romans 15:14, where Paul made the judgment that the Romans were "full of goodness, filled with all knowledge" and, therefore, "competent to counsel one another." If you make a similar judgment about a counselee, tell him so. If you cannot make that judgment yet, tell him that too. What "convinced" Paul of this about the Romans, whom he had never seen, I do not know. But Paul was not the sort of person to make rash judgments. He must have had convincing evidence that led him to make that pronouncement.[2] You will know whether you think that the counselee has the "goodness" (loving concern for others) and "knowledge" of God's will in God's Word that will make him

---

1 There are many such passages; you may have favorites of your own that you may wish to use. But, whatever passages you use, you ought to have them at your fingertips for all such occasions. See *Breaking Through,* page 98ff., for information regarding the study and use of Scripture in counseling.
2 In Paul's case, at least some of his intelligence about the Roman church may have come by divine revelation (v. 15ᶜ).

"competent" to counsel others. Your knowledge will come from the time that you have spent with him in counseling, analyzing his life, helping him change, and assessing his attitudes[1] and capabilities.

In Romans 15:13, mentioned above, the attitude of abundant hope that God wants all counselees to have is said to be the result of the "power of the Holy Spirit" at work in him. But the Spirit doesn't work immediately; He works through means and agents. Here, the power of the Spirit is not presented by Paul as something by which He zaps abundant hope into the counselee. That hope is engendered in the counselee by the Spirit *using His Word*. This is made clear in verse 4, where we read that the Scriptures were written in order to give us the "endurance and the encouragement" that we need in order to have "hope." Hope, then, comes as the Spirit uses the Bible to engender it in counselees.

The upshot of this is that the counselee must continue to spend time in the use and application of the Bible to his life. In book two, I emphasized the value of starting the counselee on a practical program of Bible study, found in *What to Do on Thursday*. This program does what few others do: it helps the counselee to move from a weekday problem to the pertinent Bible passages concerning it, then to the individual application of these passages to the counselee, and finally to the implementation that will enable him to transform truth into life. Most other study programs have a very different orientation – they focus on interpretation alone, or perhaps minimum application. Rarely do they show one how to find the proper Scriptures needed in any situation or, having found them, how to implement them in their lives. This program does all of the above. If the counselee has been started on this program immediately after the turning point has been reached, and his progress has been monitored in counseling, he will more than likely want and be able to continue after termination. Encourage him to do so.

---

1 If there is pride or arrogance, this may require an additional session or two before termination.

So, throughout all of this, the attitude of the counselee in departing from counseling ought to be an uppermost concern of the counselor. If he is satisfied with relief alone, doubtless, he will continue to fail in the future. If, however, he recognizes that the Lord has enabled him by the ministry of His Word to make the changes that brought about relief, and out of gratitude seeks to grow and live in new ways for the Lord, then he is likely to go on from strength to strength. You, as his counselor, must not wash your hands of him ("Glad that series of sessions is over!"), but you ought to care to see him go on from counseling to become an asset in the kingdom of God. You ought to do all that is within your ability to stress the need for this. You ought to create an atmosphere in which gratitude to God on your part is obvious. This, in turn, will communicate to the counselee as well. In other words, your attitude may have much to do with the attitude in which the counselee makes the transition at termination. Ideally, you ought to sketch the process of termination for him as a transition to greater joy and growth in Christ's service. That is the note to strike!

Chapter Six

Follow-Up

The concept of termination as transition must be amplified. Not only is it important to help your counselee make a transition from the special counseling ministry of the church to its general ministry, but there is additional need for the counselor himself to follow up on the future progress of the counselee. In most cases (one must be flexible since there are always exceptions) the wise counselor will want to have a six week checkup after termination, in which he meets with his counselee for a session to assess how things are going.

Checkups may lead to scheduling more sessions if there is need to adjust the way in which the counselee is handling new and old problems, if there are puzzling new wrinkles in the counselee's situation, if he has failed to do as he should or if he is teetering on the brink of reverting to past, sinful patterns of living.

If a counselee is going to revert to old ways, he is likely to have done so by six weeks. Similarly, if he is going to maintain his new ways and grow in them, he will show signs of this after the same period of time. In the Scriptures, forty days and forty nights seem to be a transition period, during which one's ways become fully established.

When possible, it is also desirable for the counselor to assign homework to the counselee to do during the six week period. At the checkup session he will review what the counselee has done. The counselor is looking for perseverance in doing good, a subject about which Jesus had much to say;[1] the counselor is also looking for any tendencies to revert to old ways. He wants to see how well the counselee has generalized the principles and practices that he has learned in counseling to

---

1 Cf. John 15:1–9: "abide," means "stay, remain, persevere." See also Galatians 6:9.

new situations that he has faced on his own. After all, this is one of the principal concerns of counseling – not only to retrieve counselees from desperate situations, but to teach them how this was done so that they may apply the same biblical principles whenever they are needed in the future.

One way to test the lasting knowledge and growing ability of the counselee in utilizing his new knowledge is to tell him that for the next six weeks he, himself, is to examine his circumstances weekly – just as if he were coming to counseling – and as the result of what he finds each week, to write out homework assignments for himself. He is then to do these assignments, write out the results, and write up assignments for the following week that grow out of the assessment of his work during the previous one. All of this material he should bring to the six week checkup.[1] In other words, the counselor will be anxious to discover whether the counselee has caught on to the idea of counseling himself from the Scriptures.

Usually, you will find out during the six week checkup session that the counselee has done fairly well in giving himself assignments and in fulfilling them, though the process may need a bit of honing. Most of the time, it will be necessary to make suggestions as to how he can beef up the assignments and how he may even more effectively fulfill them. Sometimes the counselee will fail because he has not etched out weekly homework objectives sharply enough. His wording may be vague. He may be giving himself generalized and abstract assignments, rather than concrete, particularized ones.[2] That is bound to lead to confusion if nothing worse. People change in the concrete (by doing or not doing specific things), not in the abstract. At other times, the counselee may simply not know what kinds of assignments he should give himself for achieving certain biblical ends.

---

1 Which may have to be longer than previous one hour sessions.
2 See *The Christian Counselor's Manual* for help in making specific, concrete assignments rather than general, abstract ones. If you have not taught the counselee about the difference between abstract and concrete assignments, he is likely to fail. This is an important matter to emphasize in assigning the work for the six week period.

He may not recognize the biblical connections between problems and their solutions. You may have to spend time in the checkup session working on this matter. In addition, he may have made some bad and some good decisions over the period. Help him to distinguish between the two on the basis of biblical principles. Here, you may need to help him work on discernment.[1] Mostly, these matters will have to be evaluated in terms of the way he has or has not used what he has learned in his Bible study course *What to Do on Thursday*. Naturally, you will want to check up on whether he is still following that course, and how well he is doing. Tell him to bring his *Thursday* book, together with any notes (questions or comments) he has made as he studied. You will be interested in helping him understand any aspects of the study that perplex him.

Sometimes you will discover that a counselee has begun "letting up." He has done his homework in a perfunctory, half-hearted way. The checkup session provides an opportunity for exhortation, challenge, and encouragement to improve. In such cases, it may be wise to schedule another six week checkup after the first one. At termination, stress the utter importance of the six week period, and the work that must be done during it. Don't allow any counselee to look on it as unessential. Make it clear that this is the time when final, firm rooting and grounding usually takes place.

The very thought that they must face you again after six weeks will help many counselees to remain on the stick during the six week period. This is salutary, since it takes about six weeks for a new practice to become a habit. You are interested in rooting and grounding the counselee in the ways of God that he learned in counseling. Providing a six week period for those things to become firmly established is one very valuable way to achieve this.

Six week checkups tell you much about both your counselee and about your counseling. They tell you how seriously the counselee considered your counseling. They give some indi-

---

1 It may be necessary to assign him reading in *A Call for Discernment*.

cation of how well the counselee learned. They let you know whether he was interested merely in relief or in becoming an asset to the kingdom of God. They also help you to discover whether your directions were clear or hazy. They tell you whether you gave good assignments or poor ones. They let you in on how well you communicated to the counselee the principles that he must now use in giving himself homework.

As you can see, the six week checkup is a very important appendage to the counseling sessions themselves. There is one thing, however, about which I wish to warn you. Some counselees like the counseling context too well. Missing it for six weeks makes them long for it again. Such counselees will do what they can during the six week checkup to snag you for another series of sessions. Don't let them do so! These usually are people who want to be dependent on others or who may be lonely for companionship. Instead, refuse to meet again (except possibly for another checkup six weeks hence). You will discover that this is the dynamic with which you are dealing when the counselee offers insufficient reasons for continuing counseling. You probably will recognize that the counselee is perfectly capable of solving the problems that now face him, and that your assistance simply is not needed. You may see through the flimsy excuses that the counselee gives. Through putting various scenarios to the counselee, you may discover that he is quite able to deal with them from the Bible. In every test that you apply to him, such a counselee reveals that his reasons for seeking more counseling are inadequate.

When a transition has been made to the pastor of a different church, you will want to enlighten the pastor about the goals and values of the six week checkup. You may have to help him set it up or, better still (since it will be of greater help to him), you may want to give him a copy of this book so that he will understand the dynamics of the six week checkup.

Well, you have been introduced to the six week checkup. The specifics of the assignments given for the intervening six week period will differ with each counselee. But the general aims and purposes remain the same for all:

1. To see how well the counselee is doing on his own.
2. To adjust, sharpen, and modify good work he is doing so as to remove obstacles, inefficiencies, and so forth, in order to enable him to do even better.
3. To uncover unnecessary failure in order to exhort and encourage the counselee.
4. To help pastors to whom counselees may have been "handed over" to gain insight into their member's progress.

I suggest that you never omit the six week checkup if you are able to enlist your counselee in it. If he hesitates, strongly advise him that this is the best way to go. Usually, counselees who have been helped appreciably will have no hesitation when, as a matter of course, you tell them at termination that this is the next, and you hope final segment of the complete counseling process. Please treat the scheduling of the six week session with care and solemnity; it is crucial to the church, to you, and to the welfare of your counselees.

Chapter Seven
When You Make a Mistake

From time to time you will terminate a counseling case too soon, too late, in the wrong way, without the proper safeguards for the future, and the like. What must you do in such instances to recoup?

All counselors are sinners; none is infallible. All make misjudgments. From time to time, some have wrong motives for what they do ("I've had it with this person," "I have other concerns that take precedence over counseling;" "I'll hurry things up," etc.). For these and a host of other reasons, counselors are all subject to failure in their estimates of when to terminate counseling and how to go about doing it. The question in this chapter is what do you do when you fail?

Of course, a number of questions must be considered when asking what was involved in the failure. How serious was it? Of what nature was it? What effects did it have – good or bad? Why did you fail – incompetence, wrong attitudes, or what? These and many other factors will have a bearing on what you may (must) do to right the wrongs.

First, let's consider one general factor; afterwards, we'll consider those that may pertain to a few more particular situations. In all situations, the proper first response is to *admit* your failure. If you made a poor judgment, admit it. If your attitude or motive was wrong, admit it. Though, in some instances, you may shake the confidence of a counselee by doing so, in more cases you will only gain his confidence. In the future he will know that when you say something, you know what you say is true; in other words, admitting sin and failure only tends to build confidence. He knows that he can trust you; you will not be bluffing your way through.

Admitting wrong – whether it was intentional or otherwise – allows for an abrupt turnaround. Nothing else makes it possible to reverse course as quickly. And that is usually what is needed. After all, repentance (which means "a change of mind leading to a change of direction") by its nature necessarily involves an about-face. Bluffing, even if it were not wrong before God and the counselee, does not provide the opportunity to shift course *abruptly* in mid stream the way admitting the truth does. So because it is right before God to do so, and because, as a result, it is the most expedient thing to do, always admit it when you recognize that you have been going in the wrong direction. Then shift course.

If the reason for failure was not merely misjudgment but a lapse due to succumbing to a sinful impulse, always admit your sin not only to God but also to the counselee, and seek forgiveness from both. By doing so, you will only *gain* credence in the eyes of most counselees. When you don't, you will learn something about the counselees who fail to respond that way. And that, too, can be of importance in helping them.

There are many specific reasons why you may terminate counseling wrongly. Take, for example, the situation in which you have become discouraged by lack of progress. Rather than seek even more intently the reason why progress is moving slowly, you may throw up your hands and say to yourself, "This case is impossible; I'm simply going to terminate it!" And you do so. The counselee may protest, "But we haven't really solved the basic difficulty yet!" When you recognize your sin (perhaps his protest will bring conviction), your next move ought to be to say something like this: "Well, I confess I was about to give up on you. Things were going slowly, and I was getting discouraged. Please forgive me for my impatience. Now, let's get back to solving the problem." Actually, in such instances, you may find that the frank confession of sin will lead to better efforts on the part of the counselee (not that you will confess your sin to him as a technique; you must admit sin and seek forgiveness because what you did was sin, and it was right before God to do so[1]).

---

1 You must never make biblical responses because they are strategically correct. The manipulative use of biblical actions on your part is itself sin that

Consider another scenario. You have terminated counseling before getting to the real meat of the issue. You have settled for solving peripheral matters. You know this, but you have tried in vain to discover what is wrong. Finally, you close counseling saying, "Well, I guess that we have covered all of the bases. So I think that this will be the last session." You know that you haven't covered all the bases at all. When you wake up to the fact that you have told a lie to the counselee, then – even if it's a month later – tell the counselee, "I don't really think that we've covered all the bases, as I said. That was a lie for which I hope you will forgive me. I was frustrated and gave up on you. The fact is that, unless I am greatly mistaken, there is something more that we never did get to. I'd like to have a second shot at dealing with it. What do you say?"

Sometimes, you simply make a misjudgment. "You know, I thought that we had adequately dealt with the problems that arose in your case. But now, having seen what is happening since I terminated counseling, it seems obvious that I was wrong. I think that there is more we need to do; perhaps further rooting and grounding. Shall we set up an appointment for next Monday?"

Sometimes you may be wrong in releasing the counselee to the care of his pastor. Not that that is not the ideal – it is a counselee's shepherd who ought to be caring for him. But often the shepherd is ill-prepared to care for his sheep or, what is worse, turns out to be a wolf in shepherd's clothing! In the former case, you may have to offer more help to the counselee or his pastor, or to both. You may have to say to the pastor in a congenial manner, "I probably should have stayed with your counselee and you for a little while longer. Do you want to come back for a few more weeks?"

In the latter case, there is no reason you should have worked with a false shepherd or released the counselee into his

---

must be repented of! But that is not to say that doing the right thing before God and man does not often bring good results. Indeed, though this does not excuse it, God may use your sin and repentance to further righteousness.

"care" (unless, for some reason, you were deceived by him). It may be out of fear that you would be labeled a "sheep stealer" in your community that you sent the wandering sheep who came for help back to the wolf. But there is no way to excuse that. When your conscience gets the better of your fear, you will have to call up the sheep, tell him about your failure, and urge him to leave the congregation that teaches heresy and/or unbelief. No counselor who really cares for a counselee he has been helping as he should can rightly send him back to a "pastor" who really devours the flock. As a part of his counseling, since it always must be biblical in all ways, he must alert the counselee to the danger of remaining under the "care" of a false shepherd. He must do all that he can to get the counselee to move to a church that is truly biblical. This is an essential part of the transition/termination process. The apostles didn't send those they dealt with back to the apostate Jewish synagogues; rather, they formed them into churches of the Lord Jesus Christ.[1]

Then there are cases in which the counselee may persuade the counselor (against his better judgment) that it is time to terminate counseling. When it becomes obvious to all that this was a sad mistake – subsequent activity makes it clear – then the counselor should do two things. One is to admit that he was wrong in allowing himself to be persuaded against his own better judgment. The second is to tell the counselee to resume counseling and then make it plain that he will not be persuaded again. It would be wrong to upbraid the counselee about the matter since he isn't the one who is in charge of the counseling session (see also page 31ff.); it was weakness on the part of the counselor that led to the debacle.

In other instances, the counselee may attempt to persuade the counselor to terminate, and when he refuses, then may simply terminate it himself by refusing to attend more sessions.

---

1 The situation in New Testament times parallels ours in which people from the many apostate, liberal mainline churches must be encouraged to unite with Bible-believing churches instead.

Then he may get into trouble and come begging for more counsel. How does the counselor handle that? He does at least two things: he expresses thankfulness that the counselee is willing to admit he was wrong, and then he encourages the counselee to get back to work and do *all* that is necessary to solve the problem God's way. In addition, of course, he will learn from this to be careful not to be persuaded against his will in the future.

So admission of failure, seeking forgiveness when necessary, resuming counseling in order to complete what was left unfinished, and giving proper encouragement are the basic ingredients in the mix of recovering from failure in the area of termination. Think about these matters carefully; you may recognize that over the past year or so of counseling, you have not always terminated cases as you should. If the lives of counselees have been adversely affected by this misjudgment, why not phone them today and say something like this: "You know, I've been thinking about your counseling case and I believe that there are some other things that we might have done if we had not terminated counseling so soon. Would you and your pastor like to set a date for a future appointment so that we can give them a try?"

All in all, failing to conclude counseling properly may be one of the principal causes of failure by biblical counselors.

Chapter Eight
Abrupt Termination May Be Essential

I have spoken about abrupt termination when it is wrong because of the counselee's failure to continue and when it occurs because of various insufficient reasons given by the counselor. Now it is important to mention those occasions on which termination should take place prior to the natural completion of a counseling case.

The first obvious occasion is when it becomes apparent that you have not been counseling (in the biblical sense of sanctification) at all. Remember, only true believers can grow in grace, put off old sinful ways, and replace them with God's righteous ways. If, in one way or another (the counselee may admit to it; you may suspect it and by probing discover it), it becomes clear that the counselee is not a Christian at all, counseling should be terminated on the spot.

But that doesn't mean that the "counselee" should be dismissed forthwith. Not at all. What should happen is that you should explain to him that you can only counsel believers in a biblical fashion. Since Romans 8:8 is true, "Those who are in the flesh [unbelievers] can't please God," you are unwilling to help move a person from one lifestyle that is displeasing to God to another that is equally so.

What then do you do? Counseling sessions turn into evangelism sessions. You move counseling to the back burner. Up front and center is the gospel way of salvation. That, and the counselee's need to believe the gospel message – that Christ died for sinners and rose from the dead – becomes the only concern. You tell him that God has solutions to all the problems that he has presented, but that he is in no position to receive them; they are only for God's children.

In terminating counseling in favor of evangelism, you must make it clear, however, that the counselee must not *merely profess* to believe the message of salvation *in order to* bring the counseling agenda back to the table. If he professes faith in Christ, it must be for real. Otherwise, all future counseling will be for nothing. It will not be pleasing to God, actions that seem to conform to His Word will only be external (like those of the Pharisees), and, by the ensuing hypocrisy, he will dig himself into an even deeper pile of trouble – with God! Warning and plain explanation are essential at this point.

If and when a would-be counselee does come to faith in Christ, he will have much to learn, but his lack of understanding and knowledge may actually work as an incentive to act more quickly than many who have been Christians for a longer while. Remember the church at Ephesus that had lost its "first love" (Revelation 2:4). That first love led to a zeal to please God by doing His will and eventuated in the "deeds that you did at first," works that flowed from it. Take advantage, then, of this early enthusiasm. You may find it more difficult to arouse later on.

There are other reasons to terminate counseling abruptly. One of these that is most regrettable is when the counselee utterly refuses to do God's will. The termination in this case will again be a transition. It will transition to church discipline. Remember, no one is disciplined for just any sin; he is disciplined only for refusing to repent and forsake a sin. It is persistent refusal – contumacy – over *any* matter that ultimately leads to putting him out of the church. Contumacy consists of rejecting the authority of Christ as it is expressed in His Word and administered by His church. This authority must not be taken lightly. Ours is a day in which all authority seems to be questioned and much of it spurned. But all true authority is from God. When the authority of the church is weakened, all other authority is weakened as well. Listen to Hebrews 13:17: "Obey your leaders and submit to them." Nothing could be clearer, unless it is Titus 2:15[b]: "you have full authority to give orders. Let no one disregard you." The passage in Matthew 18:15 and

following is explicit: that which leads church discipline is contumacy, a refusal to "hear" this authority of Christ in His
church.

If the person you are counseling happens to be divisive in
his congregation, you are likewise commanded to terminate
counseling, after one or two unsuccessful attempts to bring him
to repentance and a new relationship to the church: "After counseling him once or twice, give up on a divisive person, and have
nothing more to do with him" (Titus 3:10). Too often, out of
misplaced concern, a counselor will prolong counseling with
such a person. This, as a result, leads to splitting the church. I
call this "misplaced concern," because the prime concern ought
to be for the congregation that is in jeopardy. Titus was directed
not to carry out full counseling or full church discipline; he was
to terminate counseling and the church's relationship to this person abruptly when there was no immediate change on his part.
The speed and abruptness in such cases is guided by the fact that
the recalcitrant person will soon wreak havoc in the church if he
is not disciplined swiftly. Those who think that they can be
more generous to him than God are greatly mistaken, and they
usually end up ruining the congregation. Schism is serious business; it must never be tolerated – not even for a minute!

Counseling should be terminated early when it becomes
apparent that you, as a counselor, are not up to handling the
problems in the case. It is right to let your counselee know this
fact. Recommend and refer him to some other biblical counselor
and pray for them both. There is no disgrace in not knowing
something; disgrace ought to be heaped on the one who *will* not
learn, however. When you refer the counselee, refer yourself as
well. Perhaps you can learn from the new counselor. Why
should you remain as ignorant as you were before?

Then there is the counselee who insists that he has had
enough counseling – when it is obvious he has not. You tell him.
You attempt to persuade him. He will not listen. How do you
terminate counseling in that case? You simply tell him, "Okay.
If that is what you insist on, against all that I have said, we shall
stop. You, of course, could be right. But I don't think so. In case

203

I am right, and you are wrong, I'll be waiting should you come back beaten and bruised in ways that could have been prevented if you'd spent the next five weeks in counseling. See you then!" While abrupt termination is something to be avoided in most cases, you can see that is not always so. Indeed, abrupt termination *must* take place in some cases. In others, it may be strategically wise to use it to demonstrate to over-confident counselees the unwise course that they insist upon. So don't despise or fear using abrupt termination when it is biblically appropriate. Otherwise, you limit yourself by failing to use an important counseling tool that you should learn how to wield as wisely and as skillfully as any other.

Chapter Nine

What About More Than One Counselee?

"What about more than one counselee? Many of your counseling cases will have to do with husbands and wives, parents and children, individuals who need reconciliation. Does what you have to say so far reach to them?" Well, yes and no. Most of the principles that I have been teaching are applicable to sessions involving any number of persons. If a husband and wife are divisive, all that I said in the last chapter applies to both. Elsewhere I have written about those who want either to prolong counseling unnecessarily or to terminate too soon. And so it goes. But the basic principles remain the same.

Now, there are a few fundamental differences that must be dealt with. One is that counselees may respond differently to the same counseling, some reaching a termination point earlier than others. What happens then? In other cases, counselees counseled together may differ about whether or not to terminate, and may strongly express and even argue strenuously about their differences. The counselor must take such things into account and deal with them.

First, when counselees who are a part of the same counseling sessions progress at different rates of speed, it is important for all who have been in those sessions to continue until termination points are reached for each. In that way, those who progress more rapidly may be able to encourage their fellow counselees and, in some cases such as when they are members of the same family, can monitor daily work by another and even act as an encourager to him.

If there is a family conference table set up in the home, for instance, it is important for everyone to be present to hear and understand the homework that may be given to one but will involve all. In that way you will avoid confusion, misunderstanding, and purposeful misrepresentation.

If one of two persons who need to be reconciled is willing, but the other isn't, then you need to have both present while you continue to seek to get *both* to do the biblical thing. Moreover, if the reconciliation is to stick, you will probably need to continue to work with *both* not only in reaching the point of reconciliation, but also in working on building a new relationship for the future.

I hope by these few examples you will begin to see the important principle involved in working with multiple counselees: attempt to retain in counseling all who started in the counseling, because in various ways it is likely that the presence of all of them will be essential to successful termination before the series of sessions will be completed.

One of the main ways in which one may show his repentance is his willingness to help the other person who is still having difficulty in doing what he ought. If he encourages, helps, and sets a good example, he can "save" counseling for another and may be able to expedite termination for all concerned (see Hebrews 10:24: "let us give thought to ways of stimulating one another to love and fine deeds"). It is not right for one to simply "run off" when he gets what he wants from counseling. It will often be necessary to make this point with counselees. Don't hesitate to do so strongly. Use of the powerful verse from Hebrews just quoted may prove helpful.

One thing you may have to warn about is one counselee bragging that he followed directions while another did not, that he has been willing and obedient to do God's will although another has not been. You will notice that tendency in some counselees. You must strongly protest against this as sin. Encouragement of another is good; gloating over one's own achievements in contrast to the other is totally wrong. Observe that except for God's good grace, no one would be doing anything right. Thankfulness is always in order so long as it isn't hypocritical, as was that of the Pharisee who prayed *to himself* in the temple (Luke 18:9–14; see also Philippians 1:3–6).[1] Boasting is never appropriate (see Galatians 6:3–4)[2].

When someone is introduced into counseling temporarily, perhaps as a witness, he too should remain for as long as his presence has any relationship to the others involved. If, having served his purpose, he is of no more present help to counseling, he should be dismissed with the understanding that he may need to be called in again in the future. He need not remain because he is not there for any other purpose than to give some testimony at a certain point about a specific matter. He may not even know why the testimony is needed, or what the counselor and counselees intend to do with it. He is not a counselee.

On the other hand, there are times when one who is introduced himself becomes a counselee. As you can see, in the first instance, the witness is not there for counseling, so there is no need to retain him. If, however, as in the second instance, someone introduced into counseling thereby becomes a counselee along with the rest, he should continue until it is time to terminate the case. The rule of thumb, then, is to keep all true counselees in counseling until counseling *for all* has been completed.

When one is angry and refuses to continue counseling while the other is anxious to continue (this happens most often in the case of a husband and wife but also occurs between other family members), then it will be important to help the counselee who is willing to remain to learn how to deal with this situation. He must not discontinue or terminate counseling because one person has bailed out. In such cases, it is still possible to bring counseling to a successful close. In all cases, it is helpful for the one who is willing to continue counseling – if for no other reason than to learn what his role as a Christian now must be in the

---

1 His "prayer" was not a prayer at all; he was simply telling God how good he was!

2 Notice, particularly, that Paul condemns boasting that grows out of comparing oneself with another. If one wants to boast, he says, let him boast about how he has improved over what he was in the past – all the while, of course, giving the credit to the Lord. In the latter case, any comparison that is made other than that between one's past behavior and his present behavior is sin.

light of what has just happened. The counseling will tempo-rarily take a turn in which matters pertaining to the response of the remaining counselee will be discussed before continuing to give counsel concerning the matters that were being pursued before the altercation.

Often, counseling about the relationship of the remaining counselee to the one who has left will, in a week or two, bring fruit if the counselor gives wise biblical counsel that is faithfully followed. Right responses by the continuing counselee toward the irate one who left can make all the difference in the ultimate outcome. Apart from counsel about this, and aiming for it, it is possible that the one anxious to continue might have done the wrong thing in response, only making matters worse.

It is impossible to imagine and to address all possible sce-narios when dealing with multiple counselees. But keeping in mind that you must continue to counsel all who remain, under whatever conditions arise, is the fundamental principle to get hold of.

Chapter Ten
Signs of the End

In driving home from Spartanburg, South Carolina, I always welcome the sight of a very tall pole on the top of which is a lighted Citgo sign. That's not because I relish seeing Citgo signs; I am delighted to see it because of the special meaning that it has for me. I know that when I see that sign, the very next exit off of Route 26 is mine. The sign is not just a gasoline station's sign to me; it is the sign that I am almost home.

Jesus often spoke about signs. He declared that an evil and adulterous generation seeks signs other than those that God will give them. He spoke of knowing the signs of coming weather, but failing to know the signs of the times. And He declared that the surrounding of Jerusalem by the Roman army was the sign that the city and the temple would be destroyed. Signs like these are indications that something is about to happen. Like the budding of the fig tree Jesus alluded to, which forecasts the coming of spring, signs of this sort look forward to some event.

There also are signs that indicate it is about time to terminate counseling. When I see one or more of them I become aware that, if I am reading the signs correctly, it will not be long before I should terminate sessions. What are some such signs?

I would sum up those signs something like this. When I see that the counselee has solved his major *problems*, has understood the major *passages* that were applied to it, has replaced sinful habits with major biblical *practices,* and has been able to generalize the major *principles* he has learned, I realize that either he has arrived or is about to arrive at the termination point. Let's consider each of those elements separately.

First, however, notice my use of the word "major." I certainly do not think that a counselor can expect completeness in any area. If the counselor understands his Bible, he will know that perfection, in this life, is impossible. A counselee may make great strides, but he will always have many things to do when counseling ends. One of the things to remind every counselee about is that successes in counseling merely provide him the opportunity to make greater strides in his Christian life in days to come. The logs have not all floated down the river; counseling has only broken the logjam. To settle down after termination is to do exactly the opposite from what counseling was intended to help him do.

Counseling, remember, is but a hiatus in the course of normal Christian growth and sanctification. It is stepping aside from the works of general sanctification, which involve the normal pursuit of the Spirit's fruit,[1] to engage in some specialized aspect of sanctification in which he and a counselor untie a knot in his life.

So, in counseling, efforts are *focused*. They concentrate upon the fundamental problem. Many other matters must be ignored (even though some of them may be readily apparent to the counselor) in order to focus upon those that occasioned counseling. Ideally, when one is dismissed from counseling, he goes back to his normal life more able to conduct the pursuit of spiritual fruit in which all Christians ought to be engaged. Counselors who think that every problem that is encountered in the course of counseling must be solved before terminating counseling make a great mistake. They have a mistaken view of counseling itself, overestimate its value, or try to do what it really must take a lifetime (and ultimately, glorification) to achieve. Inflated views of the nature and place of counseling, therefore, can be very harmful to both counselor and counselee alike. That is why I have tried to emphasize this fact by the use of the term *major* throughout.

The first sign that counseling is nearing termination is that the counselee has solved his major problems; those that occasioned counseling or those underlying problems that were uncovered soon thereafter and that constituted the logjam in his life. If pornography was this problem, and by now the counselee

---

1 See the *Theology of Counseling* for more on the pursuit of spiritual fruit.

has been able to overcome it God's way (according to I Corinthians 7ff.), that is a major advance on the way to termination. Since this dynamic ought to be obvious, I shall not belabor it.

The second sign is that the counselee has come to an understanding of the major passages of Scripture that have been used in dealing with the major problems. Progress of this sort is largely dependent on the ability of the counselor to "open" the Scriptures for the counselee, as Jesus did on the road to Emmaus (Luke 24:27, 32). When a counselee's progress in replacing sinful ways with biblical ones depends on the Bible, and not on the ideas of man (even a biblical counselor), the counselee becomes dependent on God and His Word. That is the ideal. We want the counselee to know and be able to articulate, biblically, what *God* has done for him, together with why and how. He can only know this for sure when he understands what the Bible teaches about his problem.

The third sign is seeing the new, biblical practices incorporated into the counselee's life as new habits. They may not have so fully replaced the old ways that there is no chance of retrogression, as we have seen, but they should have begun to influence him sufficiently that his first response to a situation calls forth the new, and not the old, ways. If he is not habituated fully, the habituation process at least should have begun and progressed far enough that it now dominates his responses. This will be known by the counselor not only by what the counselee says about it, but by his relating in detail incidents in which he has responded biblically. It is best when others also can report this behavior as well; a wife may recall incidents in which she has seen and heard the new responses in actual life situations. Otherwise, the counselee may tend to exaggerate the progress that he has made, whether intentionally or not. When you have only his word for it, precise probing usually will uncover possible exaggerations: "When you heard your boss say that, precisely what did you say in response? Let me hear the tone of voice in which you said it."

Finally, the fourth sign is the generalization of major biblical principles[1] to similar situations. That means that the counselee has gotten such a firm grasp of the biblical principles that he used in breaking the logjam that he is able to use those principles in other situations as well. Reports of his ability to do this are important. If, for instance, he has learned that when facing an angry person he must give a "soft answer" (Proverbs 15:1) and has done so in circumstances both at home and at work, that is good progress for a person who used to get into contention with others all the time. When he is able to report such changed behavior (or others are able to report it about him), he is surely nearing the termination point. He will have to be able to use these principles on his own in the future after counseling is terminated. If he doesn't learn to do that, he will find himself back in counseling again and again. For your sake, as well as for his, you will want to do all that you can to avoid this. Learning to apply principles in various new situations is, therefore, essential.

In particular cases, one or more additional signs may be necessary to determine that the final exit from the freeway lies just ahead. But in general, when these four signs appear, you know that you are passing the Citgo sign! Look for them. If you have been counseling long enough to know when you ought to begin to see one or more of them, but don't, investigate what is wrong. Don't just continue doing the same things. Something is wrong. Probe to discover whether it is the counselee who is dragging his feet (purposely or otherwise), whether it is your failure to do something right – or both. I would suggest that, ordinarily, by week six, you should start to see the beginnings of at least the first and second signs. A couple of weeks later, you should see something of the third and, some time after that, the fourth. If you have *not* seen them, ask questions like: "Have I explained Scripture adequately? Has the counselee overcome the problem in several life situations?" There may be one or two knots that have become more stubbornly tied than the rest. In untying the knot, did you unintentionally cause him to knot the

---

1 Understood *as principles.*

line in new places? In other words, it isn't right to guess at progress or at what is impeding it; rather, there must be actual instances of progress that both you and the counselee agree are signs of progress that head directly toward termination.

Chapter Eleven
Formatting Termination

At the conclusion of the final counseling session it is probably helpful to hand the counselee a form that will guide him through the next six weeks before the checkup session. On this form, beside routine information like phone and fax numbers and the address of your office (you'd be surprised how many will lose these if you don't) you will probably want to include such things as the following:

1. Your assignments for the six-week checkup period (leave plenty of space to write these out).

2. Several of the verses that were pivotal in the previous sessions that helped most in bringing about the changes that God desires.

3. Directions such as:
   a. Do not phone or write about anything that you are to do during the six weeks.
   b. Write out and bring with you at the checkup session any things you do not fully understand.
   c. Bring written accounts of problems that you solved using biblical principles. Describe the problem and what you did about it.
   d. Bring written accounts of any failures, retrogressions, etc., and how you recouped.
   e. Bring written accounts of the ways in which you generalized biblical principles learned in counseling.
   f. Bring written descriptions of any problems that you could not solve.
   g. Bring a list of any questions that you may want to have answered at the six-week checkup session.

I have not set up the form for you and have only written out a few of the many other matters that you might include. I would, however, not let it grow much beyond what I have suggested so that you will not overwhelm the counselee.

You might also say something like the following: "Please do not contact your counselor unless a true emergency arises. One goal of the six-week period is to see how well you can do without the assistance of a counselor. If you should think it necessary to make a contact, do not be surprised if your counselor listens to what you have to say, but refuses to give you advice. Probably, in more cases than not, that will be his response. This refusal will be in your best interest, and not because he isn't interested."

On this form, in the blank space where you must fill in assignments, be sure that your instructions are explicit, clear, and detailed enough to provide all that the counselee needs. It is important to tailor these to each counselee in particular. Some will need more detail than others, some will need warnings[1] as well as directions. Some will need verses that encourage, strengthen, and stimulate to action.

At the conclusion of the form you might include a paragraph something like this:

> There are many things that God wants you to do. But remember, as we said repeatedly during counseling sessions, you are unable to do them in your own wisdom or strength. It is important to call on God for both as you continue to grow and endeavor to do His will during these six weeks. You have not "graduated" from Christ's school, the church. You have merely made a transition from counseling (a period of special effort to solve problems that hinder spiritual growth) to the general ministry of the Word at your church. Nothing could be more important than for you to continue and complete the course of study that you have been pursuing in *What to Do on Thursday*, to attend the preaching of the Word regularly, to

---

1 For some counselees it might be important to include a session titled "Warnings" or "Things to Avoid."

study your Bible daily and to fellowship with nurturing and helpful believers. Be sure that you continue in these things. Otherwise, all of the
advances that you have made in counseling may
turn out to be in vain.

Forms are best used with explanation. Be sure to go over the
form at the last session so that the counselee understands it. Let
him read over it silently as you read over it verbally. Then ask,
"Is there anything about this that you don't quite understand?
Now is the time to ask, not later."

If there is some aspect of the assignment that you have written in the blank space that you think the counselee might have
trouble understanding, ask him to tell you what you have written in his own words. More often than you might think, you will
discover that he has missed some aspect of the assignment.
Sometimes, by concentrating on one item that stands out particularly to him, he will distort the assignment. Be certain, that
when he leaves, there are no matters in doubt. All should be
clear. Remember, you are giving him material that is to guide
him for a six-week period. Six weeks poorly or wrongly understood and followed could be destructive rather than helpful. So,
let me say again, make sure he leaves with everything understood and a commitment to do it.

I have mentioned commitment in the first book, *Getting
Started* (page 70). It is crucial to getting things done. If you
have forgotten that section, let me remind you of the five elements in commitment. They are:
1. Knowing what it is you are getting into.
2. A desire to do it.
3. Having (or getting) the resources to pull it off.
4. Scheduling it.
5. Following the schedule.
Having read these five elements of commitment over again, you
might look at your assignments, think about your counselee and
be sure that it is possible for him to pull off the six weeks'
assignments. With reference to item #4, you might have a sec-

tion on the form that you complete (or you may ask him to complete) for *scheduling* the assignments. And, with reference to the assignments that he will need to give himself during the six ensuing weeks, it would be advisable to provide, in conjunction with this, space where these can be filled in by him week by week. It might look something like this:

Self Assignments

Week One

Week Two

...and so on. Leave plenty of space. You might add the following to the form:

> Please write out your self assignment for each week. Following the assignment itself, be sure to include a description of what you did, whether it was successful or not, and what you did about it if it was not successful.

Your assignments ought to be general; his assignments should be specific, related to the ongoing aspects of his life from week to week.

As you can see from what I have written, there is much to speak about in the last session. By putting down most of these things on a form, or having left space for filling in the variables for each counselee, you will find that you will not be as likely to forget items that you should have gone over. The form, then, is of value not only to the counselee during the six-week period, it is also valuable to you during the terminating session. Be sure to tell the counselee to bring in the form for the six-week checkup. It will be of great use then as well.

One more item. This form ought to be filled in and copied so that you may retain a copy. Counselees often lose their forms, even when you instruct them to be sure to keep them in a safe place and look at them every day between now and the checkup.

There are some counselors who do not like forms. I confess, I'm not particularly fond of them myself. But I know one thing: they are helpful for both the counselor and the counselee. If you don't like things regimented, then notice that I have suggested a number of ways in which you may set the form up according to your specific needs and requirements. You will notice also that I have not designed the form for you *as a form*. Many of you will want to design your own forms, in the order you wish to present items and with the specific materials and guidelines that you want to include. Please feel free to do so. But of most importance is the form itself. The materials included are important, but remember, when counselees see a form they immediately think several things:

1. "Well, this is the way things are done." Not, "Why has he given *me* these tasks?"
2. "This seems professional. I suppose that there is real merit in doing this."
3. "I'm not the only one who needs these helps and reminders."

Those things may or may not be true of individual counselees, but, in general, counselees tend to do what they read on a printed form, and do it more often than if you give verbal instructions or merely handwritten ones. Use the form in whatever way you want to structure it, and see how much it helps.

Chapter Twelve

The Six-Week Period

If termination is transition, then the six-week period is, *par excellence,* the time during which that transition should take place. That it is an important time, therefore, goes without saying. Yet it is a time when the counselor has little or nothing to do with how the counselee is doing. He can plan ahead, issue warnings, give out assignments and the like, but the primary thing he does *during* the six-week period is *pray* for his counselee. Ephesians 1:15–23 would seem to be a very appropriate model for such prayer.

The goal is to have accomplished all that needs to be done to make a solid transition to normal church life prior to the six weeks so that there is nothing more that the counselor can or needs to do. His concern is to see the counselee leave behind the *special* sanctification ministry that we call counseling and return to the *general* ministry of sanctification that goes on all the time among the members of his congregation.

Primarily, the six-week period is a time in which two things happen: it is a time of testing (has counseling achieved its goals?); it is a time for solidifying gains (now he is on his own, habituating the things that will enable him to respond God's way in future days).

Now and then a counselee will want to contact you during this period. When he does, you must decide what you will do. This calls for wisdom. Remember, the idea is to help him learn to solve problems God's way without the help of a counselor. When a counselee calls, his call should be received; there could be a serious problem that needs your attention, so don't ignore it. But what you must decide is whether or not it demands further attention. There are those who simply do not want to be weaned from you. They want to be able to turn to you for help in answering every difficult problem that arises. So, in order not to allow them to become dependent on you, you must refuse to help immediately unless you judge that there is a definite emergency that would substantially upset the goals of the six-week period. Rather, as I pointed out in the previous chapter, you should answer by telling the counselee that he should simply do what he has learned to do and write out everything about the situation and to bring the written account with him at the six-week checkup.

At that point, many counselees will object and demand (or beg for) help. That is when you must learn to hang tough if you think that the request is not the result of a true emergency. You may have to explain the goals of the six-week period all over again. Remind him of what you said in the terminating session, remind him of what the form says, and so on. Make it clear that he can do what needs to be done by the Lord's mercy and grace. Ask him if he has prayed about it, if he has turned to the Scriptures for help, if he wrote out homework for himself. As you ask these things, more than likely you will find that he has done none of them. Instead, he has reverted to the old ways of human ideas and frustrating helplessness, and as a consequence, is now seeking to become dependent on you to improve things. At this point give him a five-minute encouragement from the Bible, linked with some hints (not directions) as to how to proceed. *Don't allow him to turn the phone call into a counseling session.*

Is such "testing" of a counselee good? Is it the sort of thing you ought to do? Paul seemed to think so, when he "tested" an entire church. Listen to II Corinthians 2:9: "This is why I wrote, to test you, to discover whether you would be obedient in everything." There you have it. There are times when it is necessary not to help, but to leave others on their own to see how well they have appropriated what you have taught them. Indeed, elsewhere Paul tells them that he didn't come to them because he wanted them to deal with matters on their own. Moreover, you can make the point that they should welcome the opportunity to test themselves. Like butterflies emerging from their cocoons, this is the opportunity to try out their new wings.

All, in all, there are few more important times for the counselee. He is on his own. In six weeks, the hope is that he will be able to say, "I have lived free of my former sin by the help of the Lord, His Word, and His church. I have been doing, in place of sin, what I know God wants me to do. I have not needed a counselor during this time. I am now ready to go on from here to meet and solve other new problems in my life in the same way." This conclusion should not be reached and spoken as a boast, but as a thankful assurance, uttered from a heart that is grateful to God. Make that clear whenever you may see boasting arise during the checkup. Once again, point to I Corinthians 10:12 if and when boasting is evident.

There is one word of caution to be sounded regarding all that I have said. If a counselee contacts you during the six-week period, and what he says leads you to believe that he is solidifying wrong, sinful behavior or attitudes, then you ought to spend at least enough time to correct this, to turn him around and head him in the right direction. Whether this can be done on the phone is doubtful. It may be necessary in a true emergency to call the counselee in for an intermediate session or two. But when things have been righted, begin the six-week period over again. Do so even if it was during the last of the six weeks that the counselee contacted you.[1]

So, the six-week period, rightly used, will become the most strengthening aspect of counseling. It is a time to cast the counselee on God alone, apart from all special help. To emphasize this point, remind the counselee of Philippians 2:13 where Paul

---

1 Why? Because you want to emphasize the importance of the six weeks as a period in which the counselee works on his own. If you had to step in instead, that radically disrupted the time with its purposes and goals. The counselee needs to gain the confidence that grows out of "going it alone." However, there are those that I have spoken about before who would like to continue counseling at any cost, who will figure out that this is the way to extend it indefinitely: call for help by declaring an emergency! When you catch on to what they are up to, you must have a heart-to-heart talk with them about it, and, if necessary, refuse to meet with them again during the next six weeks regardless of any "emergency." This is a variation on the "wolf, wolf" problem.

speaks about those he cannot be present to help but, contrary to what they may think, are not really alone. He says God will give both the "desire and the ability" to do those things that please Him. What more could one ask for?

Chapter Thirteen
The Checkup Session

If all has gone well, this should be the end of counseling. You must look forward to this session and help the counselee to do so as well. If he anticipates it as the true end of counseling, he will do all that he can to see that his six weeks are profitable. In this session you will want to check out every aspect of what you have done during the previous sessions to see what has remained constant, retrogressed, or grown. Ideally, nothing will have reverted to precounseling status. If and when it does you must determine how serious the retrogression is and what must be done about it. If, on the other hand, the counselee has done well, if it looks like there is no need for more counseling, then you will want to send him off with a "clean bill of health" and wish him God's blessings on days to come.

How will you determine what the current counselee's status is? You will use fully all of the forms, written accounts of what has happened during the six weeks in addition to what he tells you orally. Begin with anything that is on his mind. Having dealt with that, check out any problems he encountered that he didn't know how to handle. Go over with him what he might have done.

Having dealt with these matters, it would be good to look at any failures on his part and what he did about them. You are interested in two things: whether he failed because he didn't understand, or whether he failed to follow the Scriptural teachings that he learned. And, secondly, you will be very interested in what he did to recoup from failure.

If he failed and retrogressed, or sinned in some other way, then you will want to exhort him to greater diligence in the future, and to learn from this experience. If he did the right things to recoup, confessed his sin, went back and did the right thing, you will want to strongly commend him for this. You will want to make the point that this is what he will have to do throughout life whenever he fails God and his neighbor. But, of course, it is better never to fail in the first place.

Remind him, in this regard, of how Peter forgot Jesus' warnings about denial, how this led to the denial, how he repented and how he was then restored (John 21). But go on to mention that Peter never forgot that experience, profited greatly from it, and attempted to help the readers of his second letter not to forget as he did. As the man who forgot, and then remembered too late (Luke 22:61), Peter wrote in II Peter 1:12, "I shall not neglect to remind you continually;" 1:13, "I think it is right... to stir you up by reminding you;" 1:15, "But I also shall do everything I can to make it possible for you to remember these things...." In these verses, one thing is clear: Peter learned from his bitter experience of failure. And he was unwilling to have Christians go through the same experience if he could prevent it. These words of his show how deeply his own failure had impressed him. Tell the counselee that this is what his failures should do for him too.

Excellencies in handling problems should be underscored as encouraging. Ways that the counselee might have handled some difficulties more biblically, and therefore more successfully, might be explored. And above all, attitudes that have developed which honor God (or otherwise) should particularly be discussed.

The six-week checkup ought to be an all-encompassing session. If necessary, it should last longer than a normal one: up to two hours, so that there can be a thoroughness about it. Nothing should be hurried. Nothing should be neglected or glossed over. All avenues, if possible, should be explored until there is a clear picture of firm rooting and grounding, self-sufficiency (under God), and enthusiasm for even more growth. Only when those conditions are present is it possible for the counselor to say "so long" with a good conscience.

If he cannot do so, there are many directions that he may go from there. He may suggest a couple of supplementary sessions, designed to deal with a specific problem. When that has been satisfactorily handled, the counselee may be dismissed. But if there is near total retrogression, or something close to it, he may have to stop any further work with the counselee (unless he repents and truly desires to do better in the future) or, if there is something not adequately understood, he may agree to work with him in as many sessions as it takes to accomplish what is necessary. Flexibility, coupled with wisdom and expediency, is the order of the day.

There is little that a counselor can do if the counselee utterly refuses to do anything more at this point in time. He may give up (you can encourage him, of course); he may go off in a huff (you may need to rebuke him); he may simply whimper and whine (if he hasn't gotten over that in counseling by this time, you will probably have to tell him to come back whenever he *can* get over it). In other words, you have done about all that you can for the counselee at this point in time. There may be a time later on when you or another will be better able to reach and help him, but if you have gone this far to no avail, then you may simply have to commend him to the grace of God.

One of the frequent problems you will encounter is that counselees fail because they did not follow the schedule that they (or you) laid out at the terminating session. This usually is the result of sloppy, undisciplined ways that need to be corrected. Often, counselees allow other things to detract from the work at hand, putting them off until... But "until" never comes! They may need a crash course in personal discipline, together with proper exhortation designed to show how failure to live a disciplined life, can destroy all one's good intentions.

The six-week session is, as you can see, a make-or-break session. It is vital and should be neither omitted nor neglected. Rather, it should be done always with great care and concern. By the way that you talk about it at the terminating session and the way that you conduct it at the conclusion of the six weeks, counselees should be made aware of its importance in counseling. They should not be allowed to take it lightly.

225

So be sure that you read over the form that you gave the counselee, and continue to cover all other matters as fully as necessary. Otherwise you may miss something important. For those who come to this session victorious, you might even conduct a mini-celebration!

Conclusion

You have finished reading *Finishing Well: The Termination of Biblical Counseling* and, presumably, the two earlier books of the trilogy. In this trilogy I have tried to focus on the three most critical and, therefore, most abused sessions in counseling. Abused sessions? Yes. Or, if you want to put it less diplomatically, the three points at which counselees are most often abused.

The principal reasons for this difficulty are lack of recognizing how crucial these sessions are, failure to study and think deeply about them, lack of prior preparation for them, and hurrying past them in an attempt to finish counseling. Being in a hurry is a common fault. But those of you who have purchased and read this trilogy now know that you cannot be in a hurry. You must take the time to do things well. Some will say, "He expects too much." I question that statement. If anything, while trying not to neglect anything essential, I have attempted to slim down and simplify these discussions.

Perhaps most important is the very fact of having singled out these three sessions for special study. So far as I know, this has not been done before. I believe that doing so will enhance any reader's ability to counsel if he takes matters seriously enough to actually practice them. It is, therefore, my hope that this trilogy will serve to move your counseling a long way forward.

It is not easy for some people to change. This is true of counselors as well as of counselees. I know that. But even though doing the things that I have suggested probably will involve change, I hope you will entertain making those changes.

Above all, in these three books I have attempted to be practical. They are not merely theoretical studies, but almost manuals of what to do in each of the three critical sessions of counseling. You might want to go back and make a list of those things that you need to put into practice. If you do, and if you consult the list each time before counseling, you may discover that you are naturally making them a part of your counseling.

Well, there you have it. May God bless you and your counselees to His honor and glory.

Appendices

The following forms may be copied and used. Copy each page at 150% and it will fit on a standard 8.5" x 11" piece of paper.

Personal Data Inventory
_____ Church Counseling Ministry

IDENTIFICATION DATA:

Name: _____ Phone: _____

Address: _____

Occupation: _____ Business Phone: _____

Sex:___ Birth Date:_____ Age: _____ Separated:_____ Divorced: ___ Widowed:_____

Education: (Last year completed) _____ Other training: _____

Referred here by: _____ Address: _____

HEALTH INFORMATION:

Rate Your Health: Very Good: ____ Good: _____ Average: ___ Declining: _____ Other: _____

Your approximate weight: _____lbs.; Recent weight changes: Lost_____ lbs. Gained_____ lbs.

List all important, present or past, injuries, illnesses or handicaps:_____

Date of Last Medical Examination: _____ Report: _____

Your Physician:_____ Address: _____

Are you currently taking medication? Yes __ No ___ If so, what? _____

Have you used drugs for other than medical purposes? Yes ___ No ___ Which Drugs?_____

Have you ever had a severe emotional upset? Yes ____ No____ Explain:_____

Have you ever been arrested? Yes _____ No____ Explain: _____

Are you willing to sign a release of information form so that your counselor may write for social, psychiatric, or medical reports? Yes _____ No _____

RELIGIOUS BACKGROUND:

Denominational preference: _____ Church: _____ Member: _____

Church Attendance per month (circle): 0 1 2 3 4 5 6 7 8 9 10+

Church Attended in childhood: _____ Were you baptized? Yes __ No ____

Religious background of spouse (if married): _____

Do you consider yourself a religious person? Yes ___ No ____ Uncertain _____

Do you believe in God? Yes ___ No ____ Uncertain _____

Do you pray to God? Never _____ Occasionally_____ Often _____

Are you saved? Yes ____ No____ Not sure what you mean _____

How much do you read the Bible? Never_____ Occasionally _____ Often _____

Do you have regular family devotions? Yes_____ No _____

Explain recent changes in your religious life, if any:_____

PERSONALITY INFORMATION

Have you ever had any psychotherapy or counseling before? Yes_____ No _____

If yes, list counselor or therapist and dates: _____

PERSONALITY INFORMATION (CONTINUED):

What was the outcome? _____

_____

CIRCLE ANY OF THE FOLLOWING WORDS WHICH BEST DESCRIBE YOU NOW: active   ambitious self-confident   persistent   nervous   hard-working   impatient   impulsive   moody   often-blue   excitable imaginative   calm   serious   easy-going   shy   good-natured   introvert   extrovert   likeable   leader   quiet hard-boiled   submissive   self-conscious   lonely   sensitive

other: _____

Have you ever thought people were watching you? Yes___   No ___
Do people's faces ever seem distorted?   Yes___   No ___
Do you ever have difficulty distinguishing faces?   Yes___   No ___
Do colors ever seem too bright?   Yes___   No ___   Too Dull? Yes_____   No _____
Are you sometimes unable to judge distance?   Yes___   No ___
Have you ever had hallucinations?   Yes___   No ___
Are you afraid of being in a car?   Yes___   No ___
Is your hearing exceptionally good?   Yes___   No ___
Do you have problems sleeping?   Yes___   No ___

MARRIAGE AND FAMILY INFORMATION:

Name of spouse:_____   Address: _____
Phone: _____   Occupation:_____   Business Phone: _____
Spouse's Age: _____   Education (yrs.):_____   Religion: _____
Is spouse willing to come for counseling? Yes _____   No _____   Uncertain _____
Have you ever been separated? Yes _____   No ___   When? from _____   to_____
Have either of you ever filed for divorce? Yes_____   No _____   When?_____
Date of marriage: _____   Ages when married: Husband_____   Wife _____
How long did you know your spouse before marriage? _____
Length of steady dating with spouse: _____   Length of engagement: _____
Give brief information about any previous marriages: _____
_____

INFORMATION ABOUT CHILDREN:

PM*	Name	Age	Sex	Living Y/N	Education in years	Marital Status	Living w/ you? Y/N

* Check column if child is by previous marriage of either spouse.
If you were reared by anyone other than your own parents, briefly explain: _____
_____

How many older brothers_____   sisters _____   do you have?
How many younger brothers _____   sisters _____   do you have?

231

Appendix 1: Personal Data Inventory

1. What is the main problem as you see it (What brings you here)? _____

_____
_____
_____
_____
_____
_____
_____
_____
_____
_____
_____

2. What have you done about it? _____

_____
_____
_____
_____
_____
_____
_____
_____
_____
_____
_____

3. What do you want us to do about it? _____

_____
_____
_____
_____
_____
_____
_____
_____
_____
_____
_____

4. What further information about yourself should we know?_____

_____
_____
_____
_____
_____
_____
_____
_____
_____
_____

Counseling Agreement

Have you been having trouble? Don't know what to do or where to turn? The pastors of
_____ Church of _____, _____ want you to know that they are available to take a limited number of counseling cases from outside the congregation in addition to those they are conducting at any given time. You may apply for help by phoning _____.

There are, however, several conditions upon which outside counseling cases will be initiated. They are as follows:

1. Counseling of members of _____ Church always takes precedence over all outside counseling.
2. Counseling will be done by a pastor or by one of the elders of the church; such decisions will be made by the pastors.
3. Congregational elders may be asked to participate with one of the pastors as part of the counseling team.
4. All counseling will be conducted in accordance with the pastor's understanding of the Scriptures. Your counseling will be biblical, pastoral counseling in which the Scriptures are in all cases the final authority. If you are not sure that you will be interested in biblically-based counseling, you will be given the option of attending one or two sessions to discover what biblical counseling is like. If you are unwilling to use the Bible as the final authority in counseling, sessions will be terminated.
5. If you are a member of another church, it will be necessary for your pastor to accompany you to counseling sessions. This is important since we want to recognize and respect the authority and the discipline of other congregations. And, in addition, this makes transfer back to the pastoral care of your church a lot easier to effect.
6. At any time during the counseling, for reasons sufficient to himself, the counselor – as well as the counselee – shall have the option of terminating counseling.
7. Information disclosed in counseling sessions will be held confidential only as the counselor believes the Bible requires. Absolute confidentiality is not Scriptural; matters of church discipline (cf. Mt. 18:15ff.), for instance, under certain circumstances, require one to disclose facts to others.
8. All counseling is done free of charge as a ministry of _____ Church. Sometimes, out of gratitude, one may wish to express his thanks in a tangible way. In such cases, checks should be made out to the church, not in a pastor's name.
9. It should be understood that biblical counseling consists of the giving of scriptural advice and the practical application of the same to each individual. Yet the counselee is held fully responsible for how he implements that advice.

We are confident that the Bible has all of the information necessary for life and godliness. There are no problems between persons that the Bible fails to address either in general or specific principles. While our counselors do not pretend to know all there is to know about biblical teaching and its application to life, nevertheless, they do know much and will do their utmost to help you.

Counselors will honestly tell you if they are stymied and will seek help.

If you are interested in counseling, kindly sign below as indicated.

I have read the conditions for counseling set forth in this brochure and agree to enter into counseling in accordance with them:

Signed _____ Date_____

233

Weekly Counseling Record

Counselor's initials

Name _____   Date_____

Session No._____   AGENDA

Evaluation of Last Week's Homework

Drift of the Session